Letts

GCSE

RELIGIOUS STUDIES

Revise GCSE

Religious Studies

Author - Catherine Lane

Contents

4 Social issues

5 Justice and global issues

6 Philosophical perspectives

This book and your GCSE course

	AQA A	AQA B	AQA C	EDEXCEL A	
Syllabus number	3061/3066	3062/3067	3063/3068	1480/1481	
Modular tests	None	2 x 105 mins 50%	None	2 x 2 hours 50% each	
Terminal papers	2 x 90 mins 40% each		2 x 90 mins 40% each	2 x 90 mins 40% each	
Coursework	2 x 1500 words 20%		2 x 1500 words 20%	2 x 1500 words 20%	
		SPECIFICATION REFERENCE NUMBERS			
Christian beliefs	1.1		1.1	1.1	
Christian authority	1.2		1.2	1.2	
Christian organisation	1.3		1.3	1.3	
Christian practice	1.4		1.4	1.4	
Mark's Gospel	2.1, 2.2, 2.3, 2.4, 2.5, 2.6		2.1, 2.2, 2.3, 2.4, 2.5, 2.6	2.1, 2.2, 2.3, 2.4, 2.5, 2.6	
Christian life and the Synoptic Gospels	2.1, 2.2, 2.3, 2.4, 2.5, 2.6, 2.7, 2.8		2.1, 2.2, 2.3, 2.4, 2.5, 2.6, 2.7, 2.8	2.1, 2.2, 2.3, 2.4, 2.5, 2.6, 2.7, 2.8	
Personal issues	3.1, 3.2, 3.3, 3.4		3.1, 3.2, 3.3, 3.4	3.1, 3.2, 3.3, 3.4	
Social issues	4.1, 4.2, 4.3		4.1, 4.2, 4.3	4.1, 4.2, 4.3	
Justice and global issues	5.1, 5.2, 5.3, 5.4		5.1, 5.2, 5.3, 5.4	5.1, 5.2, 5.3, 5.4	
Thinking about God and morality		6.1			
Ultimate questions		6.2			
Faith studies and ethics		6.3			
Truth, spirituality and contemporary issues		6.4			

Visit your awarding body for full details of your course or download your complete GCSE specifications.

STAY YOUR COURSE!

Use these pages to get to know your course

- Make sure you know your exam board
- Check which specification and option you are doing
- Know how your course is assessed:
  - What format are the papers?
  - How is coursework assessed?
  - How many papers are there?

EDEXCEL B	OCR A	OCR B	WJEC	NICCEA
1482/1483	1930/1030	1931/1031		
2 x 2 hours 50% each (1482)	None	None	None	None
2 x 90 mins 40% each (1483)	2 x 90 mins 40% each plus 1 x 1 hour 2%	(a) 2 x 2 hours 50% each or (b) 2 x 90 mins 40% each	2 x 2 hours 40% each	1 x 2 hours 1 x 1 hour 80%
2 x 1500 words 20%	Or 1 x internal assessment 20%	1 x internal assessment 20% (with (b) above)	20%	2 assignments 20%
		SPECIFICATION REFERENCE NUMBERS		
1.1		1.1	1.1	1.1
1.2	1.2		1.2	1.2
1.3	1.3		1.3	1.3
1.4	1.4		1.4	1.4
2.1, 2.2, 2.3, 2.4, 2.5, 2.6	2.1, 2.2, 2.3, 2.4, 2.5, 2.6		2.1, 2.2, 2.3, 2.4, 2.5, 2.6	2.1, 2.2, 2.3, 2.4, 2.5, 2.6
2.1, 2.2, 2.3, 2.4, 2.5, 2.6, 2.7, 2.8	2.1, 2.2, 2.3, 2.4, 2.5, 2.6, 2.7, 2.8		2.1, 2.2, 2.3, 2.4, 2.5, 2.6, 2.7, 2.8	2.1, 2.2, 2.3, 2.4, 2.5, 2.6, 2.7, 2.8
3.1, 3.2, 3.3, 3.4	3.1, 3.2, 3.3, 3.4	3.1, 3.2, 3.3, 3.4	3.1, 3.2, 3.3, 3.4	3.1, 3.2, 3.3, 3.4
4.1, 4.2, 4.3	4.1, 4.2, 4.3		4.1, 4.2, 4.3	4.1, 4.2, 4.3
5.1, 5.2, 5.3, 5.4	5.1, 5.2, 5.3, 5.4		5.1, 5.2, 5.3, 5.4	5.1, 5.2, 5.3, 5.4
		6.1		
		6.2		
		6.3		
		6.4		

www.aqa.org.uk, www.ocr.org.uk, www.edexcel.org.uk, www.wjec.co.uk, www.ccea.org.uk

Preparing for the examination

Planning your study

It is best to adopt a systematic approach to the GCSE at the beginning of your course, using this guide to supplement and consolidate your learning throughout and using it again as a final revision aid.

- After completing a topic at school or college, go through the topic again in the Letts GCSE study guide. **Identify the main points** with a highlighter or copy them into a revision notebook for extra reference.
- Set yourself a **series of questions** on the main points. A good way to do this is to turn the sentence into a question. For example: 'There are seven sacraments in the Roman Catholic and Orthodox Churches' becomes 'How many sacraments are there in the Roman Catholic and Orthodox Churches?'
- Answer the questions.
- From the list of answers you have, try to reconstruct the questions.
- From the list of answers, **make a list of key words** and write them onto small cards.
- Look at the key words and remember everything you can connect with the key word.

Preparing a revision programme

Your examination will be in mid-June so, at the beginning of March, make sure you go through the study guide and identify all the topics you need to revise.

- Make yourself a **weekly planner** and divide up the hours and weeks you will devote to your revision.
- Be realistic about how much time you need – some topics need more than others.
- Use the **examiner's advice** in the guide to be sure you are word perfect on key areas that are identified.
- If there are topics you don't understand or can't do, make sure you get extra help from your **teacher** or from a **website** identified in this guide.
- Study the **sample questions** in the book and understand the assessment objectives and the best way to tackle questions.
- Make sure you do the **practice questions** and include all the points given in the suggested answers, as this will be extra learning that you can use.
- Ask your teacher if you can look at the exam papers for the last three or four years and check that you can do all the questions, making sure you understand the rubric (how many questions to do from each section).
- Learn from your mock examination how long each section of the paper takes you.

There are many options in Religious Studies. Each syllabus has a range of papers to give students the opportunity to study issues and beliefs that interest them. Check carefully the paper you are studying with your teacher or by accessing the website for the exam board and downloading the details.

Assessment objectives

You will be more successful in Religious Studies if you understand the assessment objectives. These objectives test that you have reached the required standard in **knowledge**, **understanding** and **evaluation** of religion. You will learn facts about religion and you will learn from studying religion about how it affects everyday life. You must be able to apply knowledge to understand and evaluate contemporary issues.

Candidates must demonstrate their ability to:

AO1 recall, select, organise and deploy knowledge of the syllabus content

AO2 describe, analyse and explain the relevance and application of a religion or religions

AO3 evaluate different responses to religious and moral issues, using relevant evidence and argument

The objectives overlap and AO1 is part of the other two.

Coursework

Most syllabuses require two pieces of coursework of 1500 words. Make sure you understand the assessment objective weighting in these by asking your teacher and getting a clear **mark scheme**. Make sure you meet the **deadline** and don't leave the work until the end when you will have too much to do and will need time for planned revision. When you are required to do independent research, do it. Use the **libraries** and the **Internet** where you will find plenty of resources.

Useful websites

There are many websites that will give you advice and information to help you with your studies. Be careful that you do not waste time with topics that are not on your syllabus. Many websites are maintained by religious organisations and the objective of these is to promote their own faith. In Religious Studies, it is important to maintain a balanced and objective perspective, while using you own religious experience and faith.

Some reliable sites to use are:

www.theresite.org.uk

This site has many links to other useful sites.

www.painsley.org.uk

This is an excellent site for students in Catholic Schools as it is a Beacon School site and supplies notes and guidance for its syllabus.

Some issues that are covered in Religious Studies, such as abortion and euthanasia, are highly contentious and there are many websites that have distressing material from groups that support different sides in these debates. Candidates must approach this information with care.

Five ways to improve your grade

1 Read the question carefully

Make sure you think about what the question is asking and whether it is testing Assessment Objective 1, 2 or 3. Don't answer any more questions than you are told to, as this will waste time. **Look for clues in the information given** that might direct the way you answer your question, especially if your answer needs to be based on any data that is quoted.

2 Give enough detail

Always try to give the detail necessary to attain the marks. Don't write essays for two marks and don't write one sentence for eight marks. Always **pay attention to the direction to refer to Christian teaching** in your answer. This means you must refer to scripture or Church teaching, preferably alluding to documents.

3 Quality of written communication

From 2003 some marks on GCSE papers are given for the quality of written communication. This includes correct **sentence structures** and proper use of **subject specific language**. Read through your answers to make sure they make sense.

4 Use of religious language

You should be able to use words like repentance, atonement, prejudice, transubstantiation and intercession **in context** in your answers, so make sure you know what all red text means in this book and can spell all the words properly.

5 Use of personal experience

Although it is not necessary to have religious faith to do well in Religious Studies, **you can use experience of religious practice if you have it**. It is always legitimate to use examples from personal experience to illustrate points, especially in AO3 answers. If you know of parish projects that take Christian values into the community or if you remember information from services or worship, you can use it.

Chapter 1

Christianity

The following topics are covered in this chapter:

- Christian beliefs
- Christian sources of authority
- Christian organisation
- Christian practice

1.1 Christian beliefs

LEARNING SUMMARY

After studying this section you should be able to:

- remember the wording of the Apostles Creed and Nicene Creed
- understand the centrality of Jesus Christ to Christian belief
- know the commandments of Jesus
- know that Christianity teaches the doctrine of the Holy Trinity
- understand Christian belief in the resurrection
- understand Christian belief in the Community of Saints

The Apostles Creed and Nicene Creed

AQA A   AQA C
EDEXCEL A   EDEXCEL B
OCR A
WJEC
NICCEA

KEY POINT

Christians are people who believe in Jesus Christ and accept him as their personal saviour and Lord, the central guiding force of their lives. Christians try to follow the way of life that Jesus demonstrated by his own life. They try to live by the rules he set. Central Christian beliefs are set out in the Creeds.

The Apostles Creed

I believe in one God, the Father Almighty, maker of heaven and earth.
I believe in Jesus Christ, His only Son, Our Lord.
He was conceived by the Holy Spirit and born of the Virgin Mary.
He suffered under Pontius Pilate, was crucified, died, and was buried.
He descended to the dead.
On the third day he rose again from the dead.
He ascended into heaven, and he sits at the right hand of the Father Almighty.
I believe in the Holy Spirit,
The holy Catholic Church,
the communion of saints,
the forgiveness of sins,
the resurrection of the body,
and the life of the world to come.

The Nicene Creed

Recited in the Roman Catholic Mass and Church of England communion services.

We believe in one God, the Father, the almighty,

Maker of heaven and earth, of all that is, seen and unseen.

We believe in One Lord, Jesus Christ,
The only Son of God
Eternally begotten of the Father, God from God, Light from Light, True God from true God,
Begotten not made, of one being with the Father.
Through Him all things were made,
For us men and for our salvation
He came down from heaven;
By the power of the Holy Spirit
He became incarnate of the Virgin Mary and was made man.
For our sake he was crucified under Pontius Pilate;
he suffered death and was buried.

On the third day he rose again
In accordance with the scriptures;
He ascended into heaven
and is seated at the right hand of the Father.
He will come again in glory
to judge the living and the dead and his kingdom will have no end.

We believe in the Holy Spirit,
the Lord, the giver of life
who proceeds from the Father and the Son.
With the Father and the Son he is worshipped and glorified.
He has spoken through the prophets.

We believe in one Holy Catholic and Apostolic Church.
We acknowledge one baptism for the forgiveness of sins.
We look for the resurrection of the dead and the life of the world to come.
Amen.

> **Please note that the creeds show that Christians believe in the oneness of Father, Son and Spirit, the incarnation, the birth to the Virgin Mary, the resurrection and eternal life, the communion of saints and the forgiveness of sins and the universal (Catholic) Church.**

KEY POINT

Beliefs about Jesus

When asked which was the most important commandment, Jesus replied:
'Love the Lord your God with all your heart, with all your soul, with all your mind and with all your strength. Love your neighbour as yourself. There is no other commandment greater than these.' (Mark 12:30–32)

The Trinity

Christians believe in the Trinitarian nature of one God as a mystery. God is three persons:

- Father: Creator, all knowing, all powerful, all loving, ever present.
- Son: Jesus, God made man, the incarnation (made flesh). Jesus is fully God and fully man. He is the promised Messiah from the Old Testament. He was sent to save mankind from sin by his death, and by his resurrection he secured eternal life for all Christians.
- Spirit: God sent his spirit to be with all Christians when he ascended to heaven. The Spirit is strength and courage.

The resurrection

Christians believe that Jesus rose from the dead and they celebrate this fact in worship. They do not all believe in the same way and explain their belief in different ways. The main difference is in the literal and metaphorical interpretation of the resurrection.

- Some Christians believe that the resurrection means that Jesus physically rose up, pushed away the stone from the tomb and was once again present, as he had been before death, and bearing the marks of his crucifixion. He went up to heaven where he awaits the final judgement when he will return.

- Other Christians interpret the resurrection more loosely and believe that, after he had died, Jesus was recognisable to his followers in the way they behaved. They believe that Jesus is present among Christians in their own actions to one another.

- For all Christians, the resurrection promises that they too will have eternal life; they will not die but live forever with God.

The Communion of Saints

A litany of saints asks holy men and women to 'pray for us', e.g. St Joseph – Pray for us; St Anthony – Pray for us.

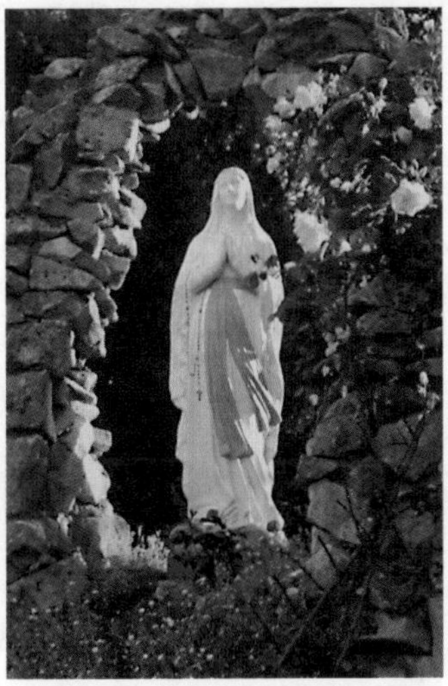

Fig. 1.1 A statue of the Virgin Mary

The Communion of Saints is all those who have died and gone to heaven. They are counted as part of the Christian community, which is the Church. In the Roman and Anglo-Catholic tradition, believers will ask the saints to intercede on their behalf. This is especially noticeable in services that include a **litany of saints**.

A Roman Catholic prayer of intercession is to the Blessed Virgin Mary.
'Hail Mary Full of Grace The Lord is with you. Blessed are you among women And blessed is the fruit of your womb, Jesus. Holy Mary, Mother of God, Pray for us sinners now and at the hour of Our death. Amen.

PROGRESS CHECK

1. In which prayers do Christians profess their faith?
2. What is the Holy Trinity?
3. Who is God the Father?
4. Who is God the Son?
5. Who is God the Spirit?
6. How was salvation secured for all Christians?
7. What do Christians understand by the final judgement?
8. What do Christians believe about life after death?
9. Which is the most important commandment?

1. The Apostles Creed and the Nicene Creed. 2. The Holy Trinity is the Christian belief that there are three persons in one God: Father, Son and Spirit. 3. God the Father is the Creator of all, all knowing, all loving, ever-present, father of all. 4. God the Son is Jesus Christ, the incarnation, fully human and fully divine (fully God, fully man), born of the Virgin Mary, and who died on the cross to save mankind and rose again to eternal life. 5. God the Spirit is with mankind always, brings strength and courage. 6. Salvation was secured for Christians by Jesus' death on the cross. 7. The final judgement will happen when Jesus comes again to judge the living and the dead. 8. Christians believe that after death there is eternal life with God in heaven. 9. Love the Lord your God with all your heart, with all your soul, with all your mind and with all your strength, and love your neighbour as yourself.

1.2 Christian sources of authority

After studying this section you should know:

- how the Bible is constructed
- how the Bible is used as a source of authority by Christians
- how Christians gain knowledge of God through personal experience

The Bible

AQA A   AQA C
EDEXCEL A   EDEXCEL B
OCR A
WJEC
NICCEA

 KEY POINT   The Bible is the primary source of authority for Christians.

- The Bible is a library of books comprised of history, biography, legend, poetry, letters and psalms.
- The Old Testament is made up of 39 books of Jewish scriptures.
- The New Testament contains
- the Gospels of Matthew, Mark, Luke and John which proclaim the Good News about Jesus Christ. The Gospels of Mark, Luke and Matthew are all drawn from a similar source and are called synoptic
- the Acts of the Apostles, which recount the growth and spread of Christianity and the stories of the early Christian martyrs
- the thirteen letters of St Paul to the different communities advising on the Christian life
- eight other letters by early Christian leaders
- the 'Revelation of John', which was written to give inspiration to Christians facing persecution from Nero

KEY POINT   The Bible is the source of authority in Christianity because it is The Word of God.

 'In the beginning was the word, and the word was with God, and the word was God.' John 1:1

The Bible is used in many ways by Christians in their worship.

- Services of corporate worship (when a group of Christians come together) will include readings from the Old and New Testaments, as well as the psalms.
- The Gospels merit special reverence and significance because they contain the teachings of Jesus.
- Christians are expected to listen to and speak the word of God and, for this reason, the lips and ears are blessed at baptism.
- Christians use the Bible as a source of authority for private worship. An individual might reflect on a scripture passage to discern God's will.
- Many Christians use Bible guide books to pray special sections of the Bible on certain days, e.g. a Bible Study Guide or 'A guide to daily prayer'.

- Christians use the Bible in small groups for prayer and praise.
- The Bible provides advice to Christians for all areas of life: for moral and ethical decisions, for social teachings and for all lifestyle choices.

There are many versions of the Bible in Christianity. The original books were written in several languages and scholars have debated the precise meaning of some of the Hebrew, Greek, Latin or Aramaic words. As the Christian Church has divided into several denominations, different Churches have adopted different translations of the Bible. The centrality of the Gospels is, however, undisputed by Christians.

Fig. 1.2. A Bible study group

Authority gained by personal experience

AQA A **AQA C**
EDEXCEL A **EDEXCEL B**
OCR A
WJEC
NICCEA

KEY POINT

Authority does not always mean people in charge or abiding by a set of rules. Authority can mean a sense of personal belief.

Fig. 1.3 Christian faith in action

People come to a state of religious belief through many different routes.

- Many are introduced to a faith as children and grow up with it.
- Some people witness the faith of others and seek similar experiences for themselves.
- Some people experience moments of revelation (they believe God has revealed Himself to them in some events).
- Some people seek out God when they find they need extra support in their lives because things have become very difficult.
- Many people are impressed by:
  - the way believers practise their faith by working with those in need
  - ways in which believers allow their belief to guide their lives in work, relationships, child-rearing and decision-making
  - the contentment that a believer might experience in trying to follow a way through life which he or she feels to be Christ-centred
  - the strength and peace that a believer finds in faith at times of personal suffering

PROGRESS CHECK

1. How do Christians use the Bible in corporate worship?
2. How might a Christian use a Bible in private prayer?
3. What does the word 'Gospel' mean?
4. Which are the synoptic Gospels?
5. Why are these Gospels synoptic?
6. How would people use personal experience as a source of authority in Christianity?

1. In regular Christian services, the Bible is read and heard by everyone together and the readings are the focus of the minister's sermon or homily. 2. A Christian might read the Bible silently and reflect on the word of God, or follow a daily guide book which leads him/her through different passages and assists prayer. 3. Gospel means 'good news'. 4. The synoptic Gospels are the gospels of Mark, Luke and Matthew. 5. They are synoptic because they all come from a similar source. 6. Personal experience is an individual experience of God through oneself or others. Witness to the work of Christians lends authority to Christian belief.

1.3 Christian organisation

After studying this section you should:

LEARNING SUMMARY

- *know how the Roman Catholic Church is organised*
- *know how the Eastern Orthodox Church is organised*
- *know how the Protestant Churches are organised*
- *understand the meaning and workings of ecumenism*
- *understand the universality of the Christian Church*

The Roman Catholic tradition

AQA A   AQA C
EDEXCEL A   EDEXCEL B
OCR A
WJEC
NICCEA

KEY POINT The Pope is the head of the Roman Catholic Church in the world.

The Roman Catholic Church has a hierarchical structure.

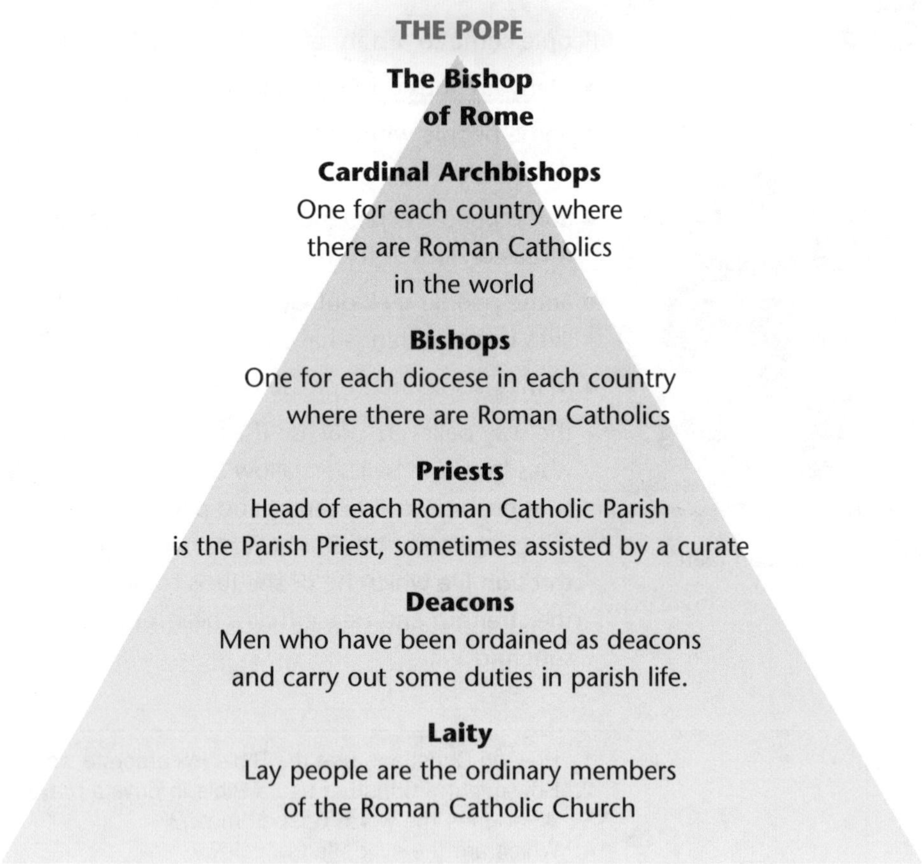

THE POPE

The Bishop of Rome

Cardinal Archbishops
One for each country where
there are Roman Catholics
in the world

Bishops
One for each diocese in each country
where there are Roman Catholics

Priests
Head of each Roman Catholic Parish
is the Parish Priest, sometimes assisted by a curate

Deacons
Men who have been ordained as deacons
and carry out some duties in parish life.

Laity
Lay people are the ordinary members
of the Roman Catholic Church

Fig. 1.4 Organisation of the Roman Catholic Church

- The organisation of the Roman Catholic Church is centred on the belief that Jesus founded his Church on St Peter. 'You are Peter and upon this rock I will build my church.' Peter is therefore regarded as the first Pope.
- The Roman Catholic Church teaches that the current Pope is the direct successor to St Peter. This is known as the apostolic succession because Peter was the first among the apostles.
- The Pope is the Bishop of Rome.

Fig. 1.5 A Bishop wearing a mitre and holding a crozier, the hooked stick used by shephers

- Bishops in the Roman Catholic Church have the role of teachers of the faith to all the people in their own diocese.
- The Roman Catholic faith is based on the scriptures, the tradition of Roman Catholic practice and the teaching role of the **magisterium** (the Pope and Bishops).
- Teachings of the Roman Catholic Church can be found in papal documents, especially the documents of **Vatican 2** and the **Catechism of the Catholic Church**.
- Church matters in the Roman tradition are laid down in **Canon Law**.

Fig. 1.6 Pope John Paul II

The Orthodox Church

AQA A   AQA C
EDEXCEL A   EDEXCEL B
OCR A
WJEC
NICCEA

- The Orthodox Church is the general name given to the Christian Church in Eastern Europe.
- This branch of the Church emerged when there was a split between Christians who followed the Pope in Rome and Christians who followed the patriarch of Constantinople (now Istanbul).
- The Pope's representative travelled to Constantinople in 1054 and excommunicated the patriarch; the patriarch excommunicated the Pope.

> **KEY POINT**
>
> 'Excommunication' means a person is excluded from receiving the sacraments of the Church.
>
> 'Patriarch' means father figurehead, e.g. of a family or a Church.

- The main belief in authority in the Orthodox Church is that no one Bishop is superior; all Bishops are equal.
- The Orthodox Church also has different words to the Creed and uses different bread for communion.
- In the Orthodox Church, priests can be married and in the Roman Catholic Church they cannot. Married priests do not become Bishop and, if a priest is widowed, he should not marry again. A man should not become a priest until he is 30 years old.

- The leaders of the Orthodox Church are called patriarchs, and the supreme patriarch or leader is the patriarch of Constantinople. He does not have authority over others, but leads them.
- Bishops and priests preside over the liturgy, when bread and wine are transformed into the body and blood of Christ.

Fig. 1.7 An orthodox priest

The Protestant Churches

AQA A   AQA C
EDEXCEL A   EDEXCEL B
OCR A
WJEC
NICCEA

- Christianity spread throughout Europe during the first millennium, changing and adapting to different movements within it.
- In 1054 there was the Great Schism, when the Pope excommunicated the Archbishop of Constantinople, leading to the formation of the Eastern Church and the Western Church.
- During the second millennium, the Christian Church divided into many branches known as **denominations**.

> An indulgence was normally granted for doing penance for the forgiveness of sins, such as walking to a shrine clothed in sackcloth and ashes. Catholics were able to buy indulgences with bribes so they didn't need to do penance.

KEY POINT

The Reformation began in 1517 when Martin Luther posed 95 points for discussion about corruption in the Church, especially the buying of indulgences.

- Luther insisted that forgiveness could only be achieved for each individual through prayer.
- Luther also put forward the Bible, not the Church, as the source of authority for Christians, thus challenging the authority of the Pope.
- In 1520, Martin Luther burned the Papal Bull (a document the Pope had published in 1302 stating that every human being had to be subject to the Pope to be saved from Hell).
- In 1521 Luther was excommunicated.

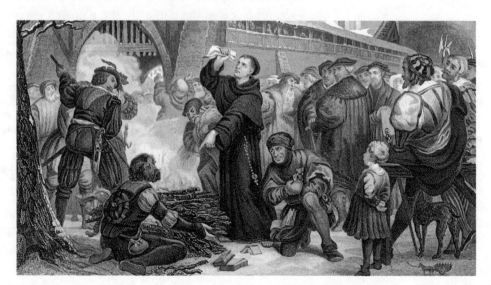

Fig. 1.8 Martin Luther burning the Papal Bull (1520)

Formation of other Christian Churches

AQA A AQA C
EDEXCEL A EDEXCEL B
OCR A
WJEC
NICCEA

Lutheran Church
The Lutheran Church spread through Germany and Scandinavia between 1521 and 1546, when Luther died. It was based on the idea that the Bible alone contains the Word of God. Luther translated the Bible into German so that the people could read it.

The Church of England
Henry VIII did not support Luther. He disagreed with the Pope when the Pope refused to annul his first marriage. Desperate for a legitimate male heir, he declared himself Head of the Church in England and divorced his first wife. Henry seized the monasteries and their wealth. In some churches the Bible was read in English, not Latin, but Henry insisted he died a Catholic. It was Elizabeth I who presided over the production of the new prayer book and established the Church of England.

Calvinists or Presbyterians
John Calvin developed Luther's ideas in Switzerland and John Knox developed them in Scotland. Calvin tried to build a perfect Christian city in Geneva where people lived, under the yoke of Christ, lives of strict obedience to the commandments, self-disciplined and industrious.
Calvin did not have priests in his Church but rather presbyters who, like priests in the early Church, were chosen from and lived among the people. (Died 1564) Knox's Church in Scotland therefore became known as the Presbyterian Church and it is this Church on which the Church of Scotland is based. (Died 1559)

> John Knox said of Calvin's Geneva: 'Here exists the most perfect school of Christ which has been since the days of the apostles on earth. Christ is preached elsewhere too; yet nowhere did I find that morals and faith have been improved more sincerely than here.'

The Free Churches

AQA A AQA C
EDEXCEL A EDEXCEL B
OCR A
WJEC
NICCEA

 KEY POINT

The Church of England is also called the Established Church. It is sometimes known as the Anglican Church. In some of its liturgy and practice, it is barely distinguishable from the Roman Catholic Church. This part of the Church is called Anglo-Catholic. Some members prefer to call the church in England Catholic and distinguish it from the Roman Catholic Church by calling the latter the Roman Church.

> 'Non-conformist' means not conforming to the norms of the established Church.

- The Free Churches were established in response to the founding of the Anglican Church. Some Protestants felt the Church of England was too Catholic and formed their own **non-conformist** churches.
- A Free Church is one that is not connected to the state or any established religion.
- The Free Churches are **non-episcopal**, meaning they have no Bishops in authority.
- Services in Free Churches are led by 'lay-people', who preach and read the Bible and lead services.
- Decisions about the Church are made by a council of lay people.

> Remember to cross-apply work. When answering a question on work and leisure in the Contemporary Issues paper, you might refer to John Calvin's Geneva as typifying the 'Protestant work ethic'.

The Free Churches are:

Congregationalists

A group of people who formed a congregation with their own elected leaders and limited membership to committed Christians. (The Congregationalists joined with the Presbyterian Church to form the United Reformed Church in 1972.)

The Baptist Church (founded in Britain in 1612 by Thomas Helwyn)

The Baptist Church is founded on **Scripture as the only source of authority** and accordingly rejects infant baptism, which has no precedent in the New Testament.

The Society of Friends (Quakers, founded in 1652 by George Fox)

Quakers take their name because they meet to **'quake' in the presence of the Lord**. They were persecuted because they refused: to attend parish churches; to accept any approved form of worship or creed; to take up arms in the civil war; or to take oaths or use respectful forms of address to social superiors. Quakers believe the Inner Light, the spirit of Christ, is in everyone. They have no liturgy, no sacraments and no priests.

The Methodists

Methodism is **founded on the scriptures** as the only source of authority. John Wesley (1703–1791) was a Church of England minister who travelled England to save souls. After his death, the name by which his prayer group had been known at Oxford was adopted for groups of people who embraced his methodical way of prayer and Bible study, which they had learned from John Wesley's preaching.

The Salvation Army (founded by William Booth in 1865)

The Salvation Army was begun **to take Christ's message of hope to the poorest and most despised people**. Booth founded an army to march out and proclaim the good news through their actions in helping the poor. They took food and clothes to those who lived on the streets and provided hostels for the homeless. The Army is organised with ranks as in the British Army and they meet to pray in a Citadel, where the Bible is read and much emphasis is given to music and hymn singing.

The Pentecostal Churches

The Pentecostal Churches grew up in America and emphasise the idea of preaching the Gospel through **the fire of the spirit**. The Assemblies of God is the largest but there are many small groups around the country. Worship is typified by plenty of exuberant singing and spontaneous prayer.

Ecumenism

AQA A   AQA C
EDEXCEL A   EDEXCEL B
OCR A
WJEC
NICCEA

Ecumenism describes all the work that is carried out on behalf of Church unity among Christians. As Christianity has grown, so have the number of different branches of the Church. Some people believe it is essential for all Christians to be united in one Church. This was made very clear during the years of conflict between the Protestants and Catholics in Northern Ireland. The Church leaders meet together regularly to discuss ways of collaborative working. The movement **'Churches Together in Britain'** produces joint statements on issues that they believe they can speak on with a common voice. There are a number of joint Church schools where children from different denominations all work and pray together.

Christians also work and pray together through practical movements.

- **The Charismatic Movement** has swept through all the Christian Churches. It is a way of worship that emphasises the spiritual gifts, such as praying in tongues and healing in the spirit.

- The charismatic movement achieved greater momentum in the late 20th century through the phenomenon known as the 'Toronto Blessing'. This is founded on a church near Toronto airport where pilgrims state they have been blessed by the spirit in a real way and they take the spirit with them to their own churches.

- **Liberation Theology** is also a movement that goes across the Christian Churches.

- Liberation Theology uses the Gospel to work for justice and peace for the poor and oppressed in the developing world and the developed world.

- Liberation Theology works through using the infrastructure of a country, influencing health and education, as well as through protest and sometimes uprising.

> 'When I give food to the poor, they call me a Saint. When I ask why the poor have no food, they call me a communist.' (Helder Camara, Liberation Theologian)

The nature of the Church

AQA A   AQA C
EDEXCEL A   EDEXCEL B
OCR A
WJEC
NICCEA

- The Christian Church is like a tree with many branches with Jesus Christ as the root.

- All Christian Churches have the same purpose: to reveal Christ to the world.

- Christ is revealed though witness, which is Christianity in action.

- Christian witness can be seen in individuals and through the work of Christian organisations, which are formed by Christians to help those in need.

- Christian help is given to the homeless, the aged, orphans, the unemployed, families and the disabled.

- Christian organisations that work to help those in need include:

– **CAFOD**: Catholic Fund for Overseas Development

– **Christian Aid**: A Christian group that raises money every spring for causes at home and abroad.

> See Corinthians 12:14–26

– **St Paul**: describes the Church as the Body of Christ and emphasises that each part is part of the whole – if one part is sick, the whole body is affected.

PROGRESS CHECK

1. What is the apostolic succession?
2. What is the Pope also known as?
3. What is the role of the senior patriarch in the Eastern Orthodox Church?
4. State one difference between Roman Catholic and Orthodox priests.
5. Who began the Protestant Reformation?
6. Who tried to build a perfect Christian community in Geneva?
7. What was the foundation of Methodism?
8. What does non-conformist mean?
9. Name one Free Church.
10. What is 'ecumenism'?

1. The line of Popes directly from St Peter. 2. The Bishop of Rome. 3. He is the leader of the Orthodox Church. 4. Orthodox priests can marry; Roman Catholic priests cannot. 5. Martin Luther. 6. John Calvin. 7. The methodical way of prayer and study devised by John and Charles Wesley and their group at university. 8. Not conforming to the established religion of the state. 9. UC; Baptist; Methodist; Quaker; Pentecostal. 10. The movement to bring the Christian Churches together.

1.4 Christian practice

 LEARNING SUMMARY

After studying this section you should:

- *know the process of worship in the Orthodox, Roman Catholic and Protestant traditions*
- *know and understand the significance of 'rites of passage' in the Christian traditions including: baptism, reconciliation, communions, confirmation, marriage, holy orders and sacrament of the sick*
- *know the significance of the funeral rite in the Christian tradition*
- *know the main festivals of Christianity including: Shrove Tuesday, Ash Wednesday, Holy Week, the Ascension, Pentecost, Advent, Christmas, Epiphany and Harvest*
- *know the purpose and destinations of Christian pilgrimage*
- *understand the design and function of Christian places of worship*

KEY POINT

Worship for Christians is the means of being close to God through prayer and praise as individuals, in small faith groups or as a corporate body in a dedicated place of worship.

The main form of worship for large numbers of Christians is the celebration of the Lord's Supper, when they break bread together.

Worship in the Orthodox tradition

AQA A AQA C
EDEXCEL A EDEXCEL B
OCR A
WJEC
NICCEA

The Lord's Supper is called the liturgy

- The priest breaks the bread and blesses the wine using words similar to those used at the Last Supper.
- Orthodox Christians believe that God becomes especially present in the wine, although its substance does not change.
- Ordinary bread is used. Some of it is called **prosphora** and is taken to the altar table.
- The rest, called **antidoron**, can be taken home by the congregation.
- Taking bread home reminds Christians of the early Christian communities who ate bread together.
- Some worshippers only take the antidoron, believing the prosphora is so holy it should be reserved for special occasions.

Private prayer of Orthodox Christians

- Orthodox Christians make the sign of the cross by moving the hand from head to chest and from right shoulder to left shoulder. They use the thumb, index and middle fingers to indicate the trinity and have the ring and little finger folded to remember the humanity and divinity of Christ.

- An important personal prayer for Orthodox Christians is a meditation using the words, '**Jesus, Son of God, have mercy on me, a sinner.**'

- Believers will also use external stimuli to help them to pray, such as statues, pictures and icons. The stimuli help the worshipper to focus the mind by acting as a constant reminder and point of reference.

- Candles and incense are also used in worship to create a particular type of atmosphere.

> Christians believed that special miracles were granted through praying through icons.

Fig. 1.9 A 13th century icon of Mother and Child

Worship in the Roman Catholic tradition

AQA A   AQA C
EDEXCEL A   EDEXCEL B
OCR A
WJEC
NICCEA

External stimuli (something to look at, hold or do)

- Roman Catholics use external stimuli to assist with prayer: typically churches might have many statues and pictures of saints.

- Roman Catholics are taught to pray to God with saints as intermediaries to the Father God.

- The most important intermediary is Mary, the mother of Jesus, who is titled the **Queen of Heaven** or **Queen of Saints**.

- Mary is the most venerated of all saints and there are many prayers that praise and honour her, the most widely recognised being the rosary.

- The rosary is a string of fifty beads grouped in **decades** of ten beads divided up by individual beads.

The rosary is a meditation. The worshipper can pray as he or she wishes or use a set pattern for praying.

- Holding the cross – The Lord's Prayer.

- Holding the first bead – Glory be to the Father and to the Son and to the Holy Spirit.

- Praying on three beads – the Hail Mary three times.

- Holding the fifth bead – Glory Be.

Fig. 1.10 A rosary

- Then the worshipper prays the decades of the rosary in order.
- The first five decades are the joyful mysteries, followed by five decades of sorrowful mysteries and five decades of glorious mysteries, which dwell on the infancy narratives, the life and death of Jesus and the resurrection.

Through constant repetitive prayer the worshipper is able to focus on prayer alone and blank out any other distractions.

Other vehicles to prayer

- Vehicles to prayer are available to suit all types of people.

> Family Fast days are observed during Lent and the proceeds go to CAFOD in the RC Church.

- There is a tradition of **prayer through fasting**, especially during Lent and on the first Friday of every month. On such days some Christian Churches encourage the people to fast and pray and donate the proceeds to the hungry in the world.
- There are also many places of pilgrimage for Catholics in the world. A journey to **Lourdes**, **Walsingham**, **Fatima**, **Medjugore** or **Knock**, sustained by prayer, is another way in which a Catholic can come closer to God.
- They may use the Bible, recite known prayers or join together in spontaneous prayer. Communities are at liberty to plan and carry out their own liturgies, including spiritual readings, hymns, prayers and even dance and drama.

Fig. 1.11 Genuflexion

Roman Catholics also have an active element in worship, symbolised by bending the right knee (genuflexion) before the Blessed Sacrament and making the sign of the cross. Roman Catholics genuflect each time they pass before the Blessed Sacrament. The sign of the cross is made with the right hand, which touches:

- the forehead as the worshipper says, 'In the name of the Father'
- the heart as he or she says, 'And of the Son'
- the left shoulder as is said, 'And of the Holy Spirit'
- and the right shoulder as is said, 'Amen'
This emphasises belief in the Trinity.

The Roman Catholic Mass

The most important aspect of Roman Catholic worship is the Mass; it is here that the bread and wine are consecrated. The Mass is divided into clear parts:

- The penitential rite, where participants ask God (and one another) for forgiveness for their sins.
- The Liturgy of the Word, where they hear readings from the Old and New Testaments, a psalm and a passage from the Gospel.
- The Liturgy of the Eucharist: the priest speaks the words of the Last Supper over the bread and wine and Catholics believe that the substance of the bread and wine are changed and become the body and blood of Jesus. This is the doctrine of **transubstantiation**.

'Take this all of you and eat it. This is my Body which will be given up for you.

Take this all of you and drink from it, this is the cup of My Blood, the blood of the new and everlasting Covenant. It will be shed for you and for all men so that sins may be forgiven. Do this in memory of Me.'

The Lord's prayer of all Christians

Our Father, who art in heaven hallowed be your name; your will be done, on earth as it is in heaven. Give us this day our daily bread. And forgive us our trespasses, who trespass against us. And lead us not into temptation; but deliver us from evil.

[In the Anglican tradition] For the Kingdom, the power, and the glory, for ever and ever. Amen.

- The Communion Rite: after the consecration all recite the Lord's Prayer. This is often called the 'Our Father' and is an essential part of the Mass as a further confirmation of belief. The consecrated bread is received as a sacrament called Holy Communion and is taken by all Catholics once they have been prepared and have received for the first time.

- For centuries the Mass was spoken in Latin, but today it is said (or celebrated) in the language of the worshippers, so that all can follow it. The altar is close to the congregation to emphasise the idea of sharing a meal together.

- It is compulsory for all Roman Catholics to attend Mass on Sundays and many like to attend on other days also.

- The Mass is offered on a daily basis in most churches, and priests are obliged to say Mass everyday.

KEY POINT — Consecrated bread is bread which has been blessed (or transformed) by the minister during a communion service. It can be stored in a special cupboard called a tabernacle. A permanent light burns in the Church to show the presence of the Lord Jesus in the bread.

Worship in the Protestant tradition

AQA A   AQA C
EDEXCEL A   EDEXCEL B
OCR A
WJEC
NICCEA

- The Bible is the basis for worship in the Protestant Churches. Services consist of readings, hymns and prayers and a recitation of the Creed.

- Communion services are also held with varying regularity, depending on how High or Low Church the community is. Protestants use the phrase High Church to describe a community that is Anglo-Catholic and has retained regular communion, sometimes also called the Mass. A Low Church is likely to have communion services less frequently.

- The way services are conducted depends on the individual Church tradition. They can be very quiet, sombre affairs or lively, with much singing, dancing and loud praising such as occurs in the Pentecostal Churches.

Protestant Eucharist

- The Communion service is often called The Lord's Supper or Eucharist. The Liturgy of the Word is when the scriptures are read and then the bread is blessed.

- The words of the Last Supper are used, but in the Protestant tradition it is taught that this is in memory of Jesus; it is a re-enactment of the Last Supper.

- In the Protestant tradition, some believers refer to the bread and wine as being transformed into the body and blood of Christ and state that Jesus is really present in the Eucharist. They do not use the word 'transubstantiation'. Most Protestants use the image of the communion as being in memory of Jesus' final gift to His people.

- Communion services are held about once a week in the Anglican Church and there is no compulsion to attend.

Worship in the Free Church tradition

AQA A   AQA C
EDEXCEL A   EDEXCEL B
OCR A
WJEC
NICCEA

When asked questions about Christian worship, you can legitimately describe the method known to you, as there is great diversity within the Christian faith and some unique churches. For example, in parts of North America some Christians dance with poisonous snakes and drink poison as part of their worship.

- The Free Churches place even greater emphasis on the Bible as central to worship. They have readings, hymns and periods for personal prayer, either out loud or quietly. They do not recite the Creed because a commitment to Christ is necessary to be a member of the community.

- Worship in the Salvation Army citadel includes traditional and modern hymns.

- Pentecostal and Charismatic worship is very focused on receiving the spirit and often includes singing, sometimes dancing and more physical contact, such as laying on of hands and hugging. Some Charismatic Christians will pray in tongues, which is a unique language from the Holy Spirit. Sometimes this is called **glossolalia**.

- Quakers have a simple, silent ceremony where they 'quake' in the presence of God; someone speaks only when moved by Holy Spirit. Believers might then read a passage, pray out loud or share a thought with others.

PROGRESS CHECK

1. What is the purpose of Christian worship?
2. What do Orthodox Christians believe happens at the Lord's Supper?
3. What do Roman Catholics believe about the consecration?
4. What do most Protestants believe about the breaking of the bread?
5. Why are Protestant churches generally less ornate than Roman Catholic ones?
6. What is the purpose of statues and pictures in Roman Catholic churches?

1. The Purpose of Christian worship is to give praise, thanks and ask for help from Almighty God, as individuals, small groups or large corporate units. 2. Orthodox Christians believe Christ becomes really present in the bread in a special way at the Lord's Supper. 3. Roman Catholic Christians believe that the bread and wine are transformed into the body and blood of Christ at the consecration. 4. Most Protestants believe that Christ becomes really present at the breaking of the bread. 5. Protestant churches tend to be less ornate because Protestantism was founded as a protest against Roman Catholic idolatry of statues. 6. Roman Catholics use statues and pictures as a way of helping them to pray. They do not pray to the statues.

Rites of passage

AQA A   AQA C
EDEXCEL A   EDEXCEL B
OCR A
WJEC
NICCEA

 KEY POINT   Rites of passage mark special phases in life with special religious ceremonies.

- Some rites of passage are known as **sacraments**.

- The Roman Catholic and Orthodox Churches have seven of these, while the Protestant Churches recognise only two (baptism and Eucharist). A sacrament is an external ritual that signifies that an internal change of a spiritual dimension is believed to have occurred or be occurring for the participant.

Baptism

> **KEY POINT** Baptism is common to the Roman Catholic, Orthodox and Protestant traditions.

- In Orthodox baptism, the baby is immersed in water, then dressed in white and anointed with oil.
- The priest uses the oil to make a cross on the forehead, eyelids, nostrils, ears, lips, chest, hands and feet, saying the words 'the seal of the gift of the Holy Spirit'.
- A lock of hair is taken to show the baby is committed to Christianity and he or she is given a cross to wear, the symbol of Christianity.
- Once baptised, the child is a full member of the Church and able to receive Holy Communion.
- The chrismation (or anointing) takes the place of the Protestant confirmation.
- The actions are all symbolic:

  The water is a symbol of cleansing from sin.
  The oil is a symbol of finding a new life in Jesus.
  The oil is chrism and it is a symbol of healing to confirm the child will grow strong in Christ.

Baptism in the Roman Catholic tradition

In the Roman Catholic tradition, **membership of the Church is by baptism**, often in infancy but sometimes as adults. Parents choose **godparents** to help guide their child on the faith journey.

- They all present the child for baptism and are welcomed at the door of the church by the priest.
- The priest makes the **sign of the cross** on the baby's head to claim him or her for Christ.
- They affirm their faith (in renewing baptismal promises).
- They renounce evil on their own behalf and that of the child.
- The priest anoints the baby with a special oil, called the **oil of catechumens**, to signify the child becoming a member of the Christian community and to **represent the strength and courage** the child will need in his or her life in Christianity.
- **Water**, which has been blessed, is poured over the head as the priest says, '**I baptise you [name] in the name of Father and of the Son and of the Holy Spirit, Amen**'.
- Water is symbolic of the fact that the child has **died to a life of sin and been given new life in Jesus**.

- The child is often **named** after a saint of the church; this provides a positive model for the infant.
- The baby is anointed with **oil of chrism**, which is a symbol of **special calling** and used to anoint Kings. All Christians are called to be priest, prophet and King.
- The child is clothed with a **white garment** (baptismal shawl) as a symbol of **purity**.
- The parents are given a candle, which has been lit from the paschal candle.

Fig. 1.12 An infant baptism

Baptism in the Church of England

- The child is brought to the font and the minister reads from the Gospels about Jesus welcoming children.
- He prays for the child and the child's carers and addresses the parents about their responsibilities in the Christian upbringing of the child.
- The infant is then baptised with water as the priest says, 'I baptise you [name] in the name of the Father and of the Son and of the Holy Spirit'. The child is then blessed and is welcomed officially as a member of the church.

Believer's baptism

 KEY POINT — **Some Free Churches and some ministers of the Protestant Churches are opposed to infant baptism and practise believer's baptism.**

- An adult or young believer is **immersed in water** and baptised in the name of the Father, Son and Spirit.
- The believer must be completely immersed as a sign of drowning to sin and being born again in Jesus. This practice has given rise to the term **born again** Christian. Even some Christians who have been baptised as infants feel it is more important to be baptised as a believer.
- This tradition is most common in the Baptist Church and in some Pentecostal and Evangelical Churches. Believers stipulate that turning to Christ must be a positive adult decision and that some people baptised as infants need to be 'reborn' to Christ in their lives.
- There is a precedent for this in scripture as Jesus was immersed in the River Jordan as an adult when he was baptised by John the Baptist.

Fig. 1.13 An adult believer's baptism

Reconciliation/Penance/Confession

- This sacrament is part of the Faith Journey in the Roman Catholic and Orthodox Churches.

- It is not common practice in the Protestant Churches, although it is practised in the Anglo-Catholic tradition.

- The different names given to this sacrament indicate its constantly changing nature.

- Originally, **Confession** was when the sinner could confess (acknowledge) his or her sins before a priest and before God. Provided the sinner was prepared to make amends for the sin, and was genuinely sorry and ready to promise to try not to sin again, it was recognised that the priest was able to grant absolution in the name of God.

- The emphasis was moved to **Penance** to show that the sinner was prepared to make amends for his or her wrongs.

- The term **Reconciliation** is now preferred.

- This is because it is understood that sin creates a barrier between people and between God and his children.

- To sin is to reject Jesus and turn away from God.

- In recognising the sin and showing sorrow, a sinner is able to find forgiveness from God, to forgive self and thus be reconciled with God.

- It is still necessary to show sorrow and commitment to change but the emphasis is on forgiveness and a loving God, not a punishing God.

> **KEY POINT**
>
> **Reconciliation means becoming friends again with no ill feeling between the people who have hurt each other.**
>
> **Penance is an action that demonstrates true sorrow for wrongdoing.**

Communion

- Communion, the celebration of the Last Supper in the form of receiving bread and wine, is common to all Christians.

- It is the main focus of Christian worship.

- In the Roman Catholic tradition, believers are expected to receive the Body of Christ every Sunday. Children are taught that they should be 'free from sin' to receive. (This used to be known as 'a state of Grace'.) Before being permitted to receive communion Roman Catholic children must be able to understand the meaning of Reconciliation. They are therefore normally at or beyond seven years of age, which is regarded as the age of reason.

- In the Protestant tradition, receiving communion is seen as a mark of adult participation in the Faith and is allowed after confirmation.

- In both traditions, the first occasion is marked by special ceremonies and followed by celebrations. People wear their best clothes and many young girls still wear white dresses.

- There is no special initiation into this sacrament in the Orthodox Church as all baptised members may receive.

Fig. 1.14 First Holy Communion

Confirmation

AQA A   AQA C
EDEXCEL A   EDEXCEL B
OCR A
WJEC
NICCEA

- Confirmation is practised in the Protestant and Roman Catholic traditions.

- At confirmation a Christian is confirming the commitment to faith which was made on his or her behalf at baptism.

- The candidate is prepared by the faith community and he or she must be capable of making a free and independent decision to be an **adult follower of Christ**.

- At the ceremony the candidate repeats the vows that were made at baptism to renounce evil and accept Christ.

- The Bishop then **lays his hands** on the head of the candidate as a sign of the **power of the Spirit** coming upon him or her.

- The candidate is blessed and is regarded as an adult member of the Christian Church.

- In the Church of England, only confirmed Christians should receive communion. In Roman Catholicism children receive earlier.

- A candidate for confirmation has a sponsor who is a committed adult Christian. This person acts as companion and guide to the confirmand, helping him or her to prepare and praying for them constantly.

- In the Orthodox Church, confirmation is part of baptism. It is not an adult ceremony. If an adult becomes a Christian he or she can be baptised and confirmed at the same time.

Fig. 1.15 Confirmation

Holy Orders

AQA A   AQA C
EDEXCEL A   EDEXCEL B
OCR A
WJEC
NICCEA

Ordination in the Roman Catholic tradition

- Being ordained as a priest is called receiving the Sacrament of Holy Orders in the Roman Catholic Church.
- Ordination is regarded as entering into a permanent state in the same way as someone making the marriage vows.
- Roman Catholic priests cannot be married and have a special role as spiritual leaders in the community.
- They are all male and only an ordained priest can celebrate the Mass and preside over the Eucharist.

> **KEY POINT**
> Roman Catholic priests are all celibate (unmarried). They can be secular or religious. Secular priests are obedient to the Bishop of their diocese. Religious priests are obedient to the superior of their order.

> Members of religious orders are either monks or priests and live in monasteries or abbeys. They sometimes run schools.

Ordination in the Protestant tradition

- In the Protestant tradition, ministers are ordained after a period of theological, pastoral and spiritual training.
- Ordination is not a sacrament and is not therefore permanently binding.
- Ministers can be married, have families and are able to divorce and remarry.

Marriage

- Marriage is a sacrament in the Roman Catholic and Orthodox traditions, and is regarded as a lifelong commitment in all traditions.
- It ensures companionship and provides a secure and loving environment for children.

See Chapter 3 Personal issues for a full explanation of marriage.

Sacrament of the sick

- This is a rite of passage available to Roman Catholics.
- In this rite, a dying person is specially anointed with oil as prayers are said.

The funeral rite

- The final stage of life on earth in the Christian journey is death, and the passing of a believer from this life to eternal life is marked by a Christian funeral service.

- After death, the body is washed and placed in a coffin, which sometimes bears a Christian symbol.

- The coffin is taken to a church or chapel where the mourners meet.

- Prayers, readings, hymns and a sermon about death and resurrection and the life of the deceased form part of the service.

- There then follows either the cremation of the body or its interment in a consecrated graveyard.

- The Roman Catholic funeral service is sometimes a special mass called a **Requiem Mass**, which has prayers and readings for the dead. During the service and at the point of committal to the ground the coffin is blessed with holy water as a sign of the cleansing of sins.

- In the Roman Catholic tradition, it is taught that some time after death may be spent in **purgatory** to redeem sins committed on earth.

- Christians believe that every one of them can be reunited with Christ after death. The words of the ceremony reflect this as they remind all present that life is short and the body must be returned to the earth; but the person will rise again and enjoy eternal life, which has been assured by the sacrifice of Jesus.

Festivals and feasts

- The most important Christian festival is **Easter** and this is preceded by a period of preparation called **Lent**.

- Lent lasts for six weeks and reminds Christians of the time Jesus spent in the desert wilderness undergoing temptation.

- Lent begins one day after **Shrove Tuesday** or 'Fat' Tuesday. It is traditional to use up all fat and sugar in the house in preparation for fasting: hence the Christian practice of eating pancakes with tasty fillings.

- **Ash Wednesday** marks the beginning of Lent. Some Christians – Roman Catholics and High Anglicans – may receive a cross of ashes on the forehead and are reminded that it is their duty to repent of their sins and believe the Gospels.

- During Lent, adult Christians focus on how they can change their lives and become closer to Christ.

- This is attempted through prayer, sacrifice and good works, such as giving alms and charity.

- Lent is immediately followed by **Palm Sunday**, when the triumphant entry of Jesus into Jerusalem is re-enacted in churches.

- The following week is **Holy Week**, during which devout Christians enter into remembrance of Christ's passion and death.

Holy Week

AQA A   AQA C
EDEXCEL A   EDEXCEL B
OCR A
WJEC
NICCEA

(Students should also refer to the Gospel accounts of Jesus' passion and death.)

Spy Wednesday	This day recalls the betrayal of Jesus by Judas.
Maundy Thursday	This is in memory of the Last Supper. Some believers attend special communion services and often the priests wash the feet of some of the congregation as a sign of humility. In the Church of England, the Queen distributes specially minted Maundy pennies to the poor.
Good Friday	This is the day on which the death of Christ is remembered. Many churches have services at 3 o'clock when the passion is read from the Gospel and the faithful depart in silence after reading of Christ's death on the cross In Roman Catholic churches these services are always Masses and include a ritual of venerating the cross, in which believers kiss the feet of Christ on a crucifix. Christians follow the tradition on this day of eating hot cross buns – spiced buns with crosses on them. It is also known as the one day of compulsory fasting and abstinence when Christians are obliged not to eat meat and to fast consciously in memory of Jesus' suffering and death
Holy Saturday	On Holy Saturday the resurrection of Jesus is celebrated after sundown and Easter has begun. The vigil service takes place and the **Easter (paschal) candle** is lit from a special fire as a sign of the light of Christ. At the Easter vigil, the faithful repeat their baptismal vows and rejoice with hymns, reading and prayers in the risen Christ who they believe is truly alive today.
Easter Sunday	Easter Sunday is a day on which many Christians attend church, even if they have not done so throughout the year. All Roman Catholics are obliged to receive the sacraments of Reconciliation and Eucharist at some point during the Easter period. This is known as the Easter Duty. At Easter Sunday services, the Gospels of the resurrection are read and prayers and hymns of rejoicing in the risen Lord form the most important services of the year. The church is decorated with many flowers symbolising spring and new life On Easter Sunday throughout the Christian world millions of people eat chocolate eggs. The eggs are a symbol of new life. In some parts of the world eggs are rolled down hills as a sign of the stone rolling away from the tomb

The Ascension

The Ascension of the Lord into heaven is celebrated six weeks after Easter. Christians read the Gospel accounts at services or Mass.

> 'And so the Lord Jesus, after He had spoken to them, was taken up into heaven.' (Mark 16:19).

Pentecost

- Pentecost, usually called **Whitsun,** is celebrated seven weeks after Easter.
- Christians recall when the Holy Spirit visited the terrified disciples. The Gospel accounts speak of a roaring wind and the appearance of tongues of fire.
- The disciples received the gift of tongues and were able to spread the Good News about Jesus to people of all nationalities. When they spoke they were understood by people from many different countries.
- It is important for Christians today that the power of Jesus was seen to return in the form of the Holy Spirit and it is this almost invisible force that many Christians are able to relate to as the real presence of God in the world. Many believers call on the Spirit prayer to help them find courage, strength and wisdom.

Advent

- The second most important time in the Christian calendar is the marking of the Advent period.
- Advent begins on the Sunday that is the fourth clear Sunday before December 25th.
- It is frequently acknowledged in homes, churches and Church schools by the use of a symbolic advent wreath, which has five candles.
- A candle is lit on each of the four Sundays of Advent and the fifth is lit on Christmas Day.
- If Christmas falls on a Sunday, Advent can be five weeks long.
- During Advent, Christians are expected to prepare for the birth of Jesus, to reflect on their own Christian lives and to consider the importance of the fact that God became man and came to earth as a baby to show His love for all humanity.
- The lighting of advent candles signifies that Christians eagerly wait to renew their joy at the coming of the **light of the world**.

The Second Coming

During Advent, Christians are also united in renewing their longing for the **Second Coming**, the time when Christ will return to judge the living and the dead (as stated in the Creed), and everything that is will be subject to Him, and evil will be conquered for ever.

Christianity

Christmas

AQA A AQA C
EDEXCEL A EDEXCEL B
OCR A
WJEC
NICCEA

KEY POINT

Christians celebrate the birth of Christ the Saviour. They acknowledge that God became man and lived among them.

This is called the Incarnation. Jesus is God made flesh, the light entered the world.

'For there is a child born to us, a son given to us and dominion is laid on his shoulders; and this is the name they give him: Wonderful Counsellor, Mighty God, Eternal Father, Prince of Peace.'
(Isaiah 9:6)

- At Christmas time in Christian churches, believers read and listen to the prophecies about the coming Messiah from the Old Testament, and also the infancy narratives from the Gospels of Matthew and Luke. They also sing traditional Christmas carols telling the stories of the birth of Jesus and rejoicing in the birth.

- There are many traditions associated with Christmas, which can be traced back through the centuries and are often identified with pagan rites of mid-winter solstice festivities. They have, however, been accorded symbolic meaning by Christians.

- **Present-giving** around December (usually 25th) has come to symbolise God's love for His people so this is celebrated by giving presents to loved ones.

You should be aware that all the traditional things we do in Britain at Christmas have some relevance to the Christian celebration of Jesus' coming, so remember to include them when writing about Christmas rituals.

- The **evergreen** tree decorated with lights is a symbol of life in the barren winter months and light shining through the world from belief in Jesus.

- **The Christmas meal** is a ritual shared by the family. Sharing food is always recognised by Christians as symbolic of Christ's sharing of his final supper with all his followers. Eating together is a sign of companionship.

- Christians also exchange cards and greetings, decorate their houses with holly and ivy and some put wreaths of evergreen on their doors as an external sign of belief and witness.

The Epiphany/Twelfth Night

- Christmas is followed by the celebration of the **Epiphany** when the Wise Men visited Jesus. This is to show that Christ came to save all the world.

- In some Christian communities gifts are exchanged on this day, January 6th.

Harvest Festival

In September it is becoming more widespread to celebrate the harvest. This is done particularly now in the affluent world to thank God for the bounty that is enjoyed, raise awareness of the hunger in the world and use harvest time to contribute to helping those in need of food.

Pilgrimage

AQA A AQA C
EDEXCEL A EDEXCEL B
OCR A
WJEC
NICCEA

KEY POINT

Christianity is a journey into Christ – a journey that mirrors every Christian's mystery journey through life. As a Christian grows and changes, so he or she tries to move nearer to Christ. A believer's ultimate hope is to be completely at one with Him in eternity. While on the journey, Christians may use the physical act of pilgrimage to help them focus on the need for spiritual nourishment.

Christianity

> This is a key concept in Christianity, which can be referred to as a point of understanding when answering other questions as well, especially issues of right and wrong.

Any place of holy significance is an appropriate destination for pilgrimage. Important destinations are:

- **Lourdes**, where St Bernadette saw a vision of the Virgin Mary and a healing spring was revealed.

- **Walsingham** in England, site of Anglican and Roman Catholic shrines to the Virgin Mary.

- **Medjugore** in Bosnia and **Fatima** in Portugal, where visions of the Virgin Mary were seen and secret prophecies given.

- **Lindisfarne** and **Iona**, sites of the early Christian presence of the communities of Saints Aidan and Columba.

- **The Holy Land** and places of significance described in the Gospels, for example, **Bethlehem**, **Jerusalem** and **Nazareth**.

- **Rome** and **St Peter's**, a centre of pilgrimage for all Christians, especially Roman Catholics.

Throughout the world there are many holy places to which Christians become especially devoted, and these vary with the times.

Places of worship

AQA A   AQA C
EDEXCEL A   EDEXCEL B
OCR A
WJEC
NICCEA

> 'Cathedra' is a Latin word meaning 'chair'. Cathedral takes its name because this is where the Bishop's Chair is found.

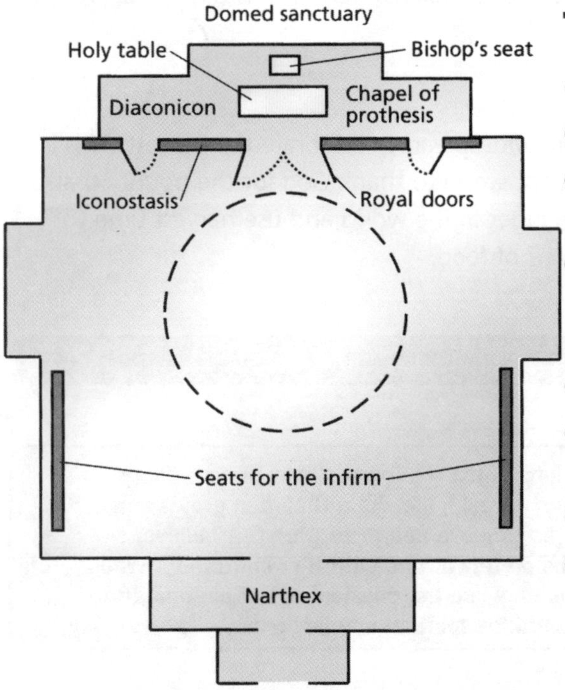

- The Christian place of worship is called a church or chapel.

- Every diocese in the Church of England and the Roman Catholic Church has its own cathedral church. This is large and imposing and is the focal point for all diocesan services; it contains the seat of the bishop of the diocese.

- There is a standard layout for most parish churches, many of which were built before the Reformation.

- Few new churches are built today because of dwindling congregations in most areas, but those that are built often have different shapes while still retaining the usual features.

- A chapel is normally smaller and less ornate. Chapels are favoured by non-conformist Christians.

The Orthodox Church

- Orthodox churches are square with a dome on top.

- The square represents order and equality.

- The floor of the nave represents the earth and the four corners represent the four evangelists.

- Seats are provided only for the old and weak, and people can move about during services; usually they stand still to worship.

- The churches are richly decorated.

- The circular dome, located above the apex of the cross formed by the transepts, represents eternity.

- Around the walls are pictures of saints.

- On the altar table is a seven-branched candlestick, which represents the seven sacraments and the seven gifts of the spirit.

Fig. 1.16 An Orthodox church building

Diagram labels: Domed sanctuary, Holy table, Bishop's seat, Diaconicon, Chapel of prothesis, Iconostasis, Royal doors, Seats for the infirm, Narthex

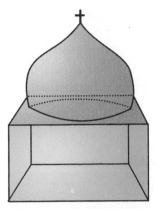

- At the entrance to the church is the narthex. This is the stage traversed by novitiate Christians and people wishing to enter Christianity.

- Across the front of the church is a huge screen decorated with pictures of the evangelists. This is called the **iconostasis**. Behind this are three areas: the **diaconicon**, where robes and equipment are kept and where the priests dress; **the chapel of prothesis**, where the bread and wine are prepared; and **a domed sanctuary**, where the Eucharist takes place. This is entered by the curtained royal doors. The priests carry the Gospels and the bread and wine through these doors.

Fig. 1.17 The basic shape of an Orthodox Church

The Roman Catholic Church

- Roman Catholic churches vary in shape.

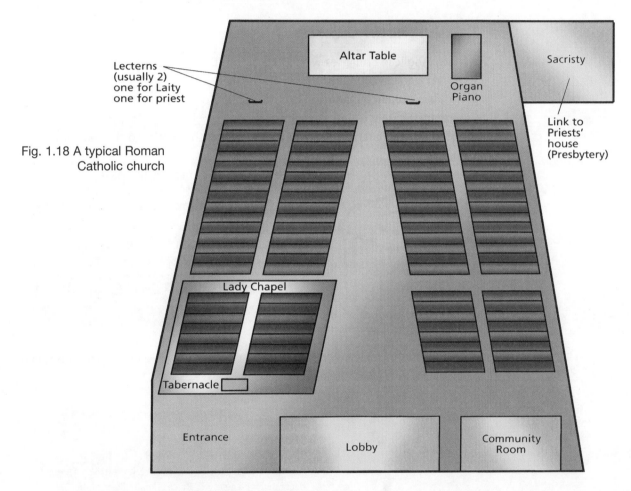

Fig. 1.18 A typical Roman Catholic church

Lecterns (usually 2) one for Laity one for priest

Altar Table

Organ Piano

Sacristy

Link to Priests' house (Presbytery)

Lady Chapel

Tabernacle

Entrance

Lobby

Community Room

- The table or altar on which the bread and wine are consecrated is the focal point of the building.

- This is the Eucharistic table, the Mass being a celebration of a Christian community breaking bread together. The minister blesses the bread and wine and Jesus becomes present in the Eucharist. The Last Supper is re-enacted for all the worshippers. In modern churches this feature is combined with some of the more traditional aspects which are important to people. There are several typical features:

Fig. 1.19 The altar table

(a) A Blessed Sacrament chapel area; the tabernacle housed here contains any consecrated bread and wine.

(b) A Lady Chapel with a statue of the Virgin Mary and a prie-dieu for private prayer.

(c) The baptismal font. This is near to the altar. Often, however, there is no font and the priest brings a bowl of water to the altar for baptism.

(d) Pictures or carvings of the Stations of the Cross. These are found at intervals around the church.

(e) A confessional (in some churches), with two adjoining rooms for private confession.

(f) A sacristy where artefacts are kept and where the priest robes.

- Readings and sermons are delivered from small, plain lecterns to emphasise that the words are important, not the grandness of the reader.
- Few churches have large organs and choir lofts. Music is communal and the leader of liturgical music sits with the congregation or as close as possible.

The Anglican Church

- Many Anglican churches were built before the Reformation and tend to remain traditional in layout.
- They are usually rectangular or in the shape of a cross. Cathedrals are particularly likely to be cross-shaped.
- A traditional church has a door at one side with a belfry to the rear of the nave.
- The baptismal font is close to the rear of the church in the nave.

The baptismal font
This is found at the rear of traditional churches as a sign that new entrants to the Church are to be baptised. It is becoming more usual to baptise people at the front of the church, where they can be seen by the congregation.

- At the front of the church is the raised pulpit from which the sermon is given.
- There is a lectern for scripture readings.

The lectern
This is a stand from which the Word is read by either a member of the laity or the minister. It is often decorated with an eagle, which is symbolic of raising the Word up to God and God raising his followers 'on eagle wings'.

- At the very front is the high altar where communion services are conducted.
- Directly in front of this is the chancel and the choir stalls.
- A cathedral traditionally has transepts and contains the bishop's throne.
- Sometimes there are side chapels, many of which date from before the Reformation and were used for private Masses. A number of cathedrals still preserve their Lady Chapels.
- Anglican churches do not often have statues or pictures, although some High churches retain images from pre-Reformation tradition.

The pulpit
This can be found in traditional churches, but it has been removed in Roman Catholic churches. It was used for the minister to deliver the sermon as he could be seen and heard, but it also established his position above that of the congregation.

The high alter
Found in older and more traditional churches and rarely used except to store consecrated bread in a tabernacle.

Non-conformist tradition is such that the churches have a much less formal design; this emphasises the equality of the worshippers. The churches are more modern and so have been designed with practicalities in mind. Many non-conformist churches are rectangular in shape but they may be organised to allow for conversion for social functions. Often the pulpit is at the centre of the front, behind the communion table, to show the centrality of the teaching of the Word of God. They are plain with no artefacts or statues.

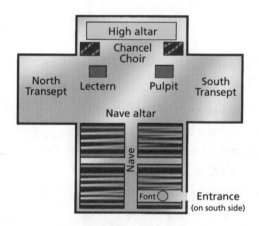

Fig. 1.20 The Anglican church is cross-shaped. The altar is the focus of the building. It is set apart to create a feeling of mystery and awe. The central part of the church is the nave where the congregation sits.

Fig. 1.21 The furnishings of a non-conformist church are usually less ornate. The focal point is the elevated pulpit, in front of which is a far less noticeable communion table.

1. How is making a pilgrimage helpful to Christians?
2. How might the Bible be used to pray?
3. What are the seven sacraments recognised by the Roman Catholic Church?
4. Why is Easter the most important celebration in the Church's year?
5. Why do Christians observe Lent?

1. Making a physical pilgrimage to a holy place is a way of understanding the Christian life journey, which is a journey into Christ. 2. Christians may read the Bible systematically and reflect on the words, follow a study guide or dip in at random for a revelation from God. 3. Baptism, Reconciliation, Eucharist, confirmation, marriage, holy orders and sacrament of the sick. 4. Easter is the celebration of Jesus rising from the dead to be with his people for all time. Christians celebrate this fact every day. 5. To prepare for the death of Jesus and focus on the Christian life of service and sacrifice. To re-centre the meaning of life on the risen Jesus.

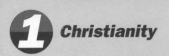
Sample GCSE questions

1. Look at the picture and answer each part of the question that follows.

(a) (i) Name the objects 1 and 2 as shown. **(2)**

Baptismal font and lectern

(ii) Explain the importance for Christians of **either** the pulpit **or** ◄ the altar. **(3)**

Pulpit: This is the raised box in the traditional style of Protestant Churches from which the minister preaches the Word of God. After the reading of the Gospel, the minister explores its meaning for Christians today. The lofty position of the pulpit emphasises the centrality of the Word of God in Christian worship. It encourages respect for the minister who is ordained to preach the Word to the faithful.

Altar: The altar is also known as the Table of the Lord. This is the table where the minister breaks the bread during communion services and repeats the words given by Jesus at the Last Supper. Christians regard the altar as a sacred focus of worship. Roman Catholics offer the Mass as a sacrifice and remember that Christ was sacrificed for all humanity. The consecration of the bread and wine on the altar is a re-enactment of Christ's sacrifice.

(b) How might attending Church services on a Sunday help young ◄ Christians during the rest of the week? **(5)**

By going to church on a Sunday, a young Christian can participate in corporate worship. Christians have an intimate relationship with Jesus Christ but sometimes this is difficult to keep uppermost in the mind during the busy week. An hour in prayer with others helps to nourish

> Note the question asks you to choose either altar or pulpit, NOT BOTH. The question demands that you explain the importance of each and you will not get full marks if you only say what the object is for.

> Be careful of under-estimating the demands of the question. This question demands explicit knowledge of Christian belief about the value of corporate religious worship and the precise nature of Sunday services. You will need two or three points with some development to achieve all five marks.

Sample GCSE questions

Christian faith and sustain a Christian in daily life. The Christian will hear the Word of God and reflect on it. Many Christians will receive Christ in communion, thus receiving special grace, which helps them to remain faithful. The message of Jesus helps Christians to make moral choices throughout life and constant listening to the message helps young Christians to follow Christ's teaching on a daily basis. Weekly church with others helps young Christians to feel supported in their beliefs and not alone in a world where there are many non-church attendees.

(c) 'Going to church is something I might do when I get old. While I'm young I want to enjoy life to the full.'

How far do you agree with this comment? (You should show that you understand different opinions and Christian teachings.) **(5)**

This is an AO3 question, which means you must use your knowledge and understanding to present a balanced argument based on facts and show you understand how Christian belief affects daily life. Do not just give opinion with no facts to support your ideas.

Christians go to church because they believe that Christ is present where one or more are gathered in his name. They believe that he is present in the breaking of the bread and they find strength and support in worshipping together. Christians also feel obliged to keep the commandment to observe the Sabbath day and devote one day to rest and prayer as the Lord did when He created the earth. Christians find spiritual nourishment in prayer and are able to experience God in different individual ways through worship. These benefits are available to Christians at any age and there is no reason to keep them for old age.

It is natural for young people to avoid thinking of church because there are many other things to do on Sundays. Many young people associate religious belief with what happens after death and believe there will be time to think about that later. Christianity teaches that no one knows the day or the hour when they will be called to account for their lives so they should always be ready. Christianity also teaches that you cannot serve God and money and should love the Lord your God before all else.

AQA (SEG) Syllabus A, 2000

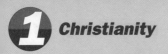

Exam practice questions

1. **Beliefs and values**

(a) State one thing that Christians believe about Jesus. (2)

....

....

(b) What teaching is outlined about God the Father in the Apostles Creed? (6)

....

....

....

....

(c) Christianity teaches faith and repentance. Explain why these are important parts of Christian belief. (8)

....

....

....

....

....

(d) 'It is possible to be a good person and not be a religious believer.'
Do you agree? Give reasons for your opinion, showing that you have considered another point of view. (4)

....

....

....

Exam practice questions

2. **Organisation**

(a) State what you understand by the word 'laity'. (2)

....

....

(b) How might a Bible be used in public worship. (6)

....

....

....

....

....

(c) Christians regard the Church as a source of faith. Explain what is meant by this idea. (8)

....

....

....

....

....

(d) 'To be a proper Christian, you need to be part of a community.'
Do you agree? Give reasons for your opinion, showing that you have considered
more than one point of view. (4)

....

....

....

The Gospels

The following topics are covered in this chapter:

- The person of Jesus
- The importance of the Gospels
- Miracles in Mark
- The parables of the Kingdom of God
- Episodes of conflict
- Discipleship
- Luke's Gospel
- Matthew's Gospel

KEY POINT

The Gospels are the Good News that Jesus Christ is Lord and Saviour who died for all people to save them from sin. The Gospels teach people a new way to live to come to the Father God through the Son Jesus.

2.1 The person of Jesus

LEARNING SUMMARY

After studying this section you should:

- know that Jesus is referred to as Christ, Messiah, Son of David, Jesus, Saviour, Son of Man and Son of God
- understand these terms and what they mean to readers of the Gospels
- know when these terms are used, by whom and why

Jesus Christ/Messiah/Son of David

AQA A   AQA C
EDEXCEL A   EDEXCEL B
OCR A
WJEC
NICCEA

Candidates must be absolutely familiar with the texts given in this section, preferably knowing them by heart and, at least, knowing the meaning of all the events and the outline of Jesus' words.

- The Gospels are about Jesus, the great founder of Christianity, with nearly two billion followers worldwide.

- Jesus is the Christ, from the Greek word *Christos* meaning 'Messiah' or 'anointed one'.

- Jesus is anointed by the woman at Bethany who pours nard (a type of oil) on his head (Mark 14:3–9; Matt. 26:6–13). Jews had long been awaiting a Messiah, which had been prophesied in the Old Testament, but they had fixed ideas about what the Messiah would be like. Some expected a prophet like Moses.

- Some Jews were expecting the Messiah to be a war-like leader who would free them from the Romans.

- Jesus is called the Christ at Caesarea Philippi (Mark 8:27).

- Blind Bartimaeus calls Jesus 'Son of David' (Mark 10:46–52).
- The crowd acclaims Jesus, 'Blessed is the coming of our Father David' when he rides into Jerusalem on a donkey (Mark 11:1).
- The title 'Son of David' also indicates that Jesus was expected to be a King. He is referred to by Mark as 'King' during his crucifixion.
- Jesus' resurrection showed he was to be the King of Heaven.

> **KEY POINT**
>
> **The Messianic Secret**
> The fact that Jesus is the Messiah is revealed slowly, and much of the time Jesus asks for it to be kept secret. Hence the term 'Son of David' is most frequently used.

Suffering servant/Son of Man

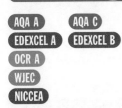

AQA A AQA C
EDEXCEL A EDEXCEL B
OCR A
WJEC
NICCEA

- There are indications in the Gospel that Jesus saw himself more as the 'suffering servant', prophesied in Isaiah (Is. 35:4; 53:2–12).
- The reference to the Son of Man is also found in:
    Psalm 8:1 where he is 'an ordinary human being'
    Ezekiel 2:1 where he is one representative of God
    Daniel 7:14 where he is a mysterious heavenly being who will bring a Kingdom
- Jesus seems to take the role of the Son of Man given by Daniel, coupled with the Isaiah idea of the suffering servant.
- He often told his disciples that the Son of Man would suffer and die. He put great emphasis on the need to put self last and be servant of all.
- Understanding Jesus as Son of Man helps readers to understand that he had the same emotions and feelings as all humanity; he felt both pain and joy.

Episodes where Jesus is called 'Son of Man'

- The healing of the paralytic (Mark 2:1–11). Jesus heals the man by telling him his sins are forgiven. He tells the watchers that, 'the Son of Man has authority on earth to forgive sins'.
- When Jesus predicts his death (Mark 8:31–33), he says, 'the Son of Man' must suffer many things.
- James and John ask if they will sit with Jesus after his death and he tells them they know nothing about what the Son of Man will suffer. They have not understood the nature of his Messiahship.

Son of God

- Jesus is not called Son of God by any human being until after his death.

- The term was thought to be blasphemous by Jews.

- Evil spirits recognise Jesus as Son of God and when he exorcises them he shows his power over evil.

- Mark begins by stating in the kerygma (Proclamation of Faith 1:1) that Jesus is the Son of God.

Episodes

- Baptism (Mark 1:9–11). Readers are told the voice of God is heard saying, 'You are my Son...'

- Transfiguration (Mark 9:2–8). A voice is heard again: 'This is my Son, whom I love...'

- The trial before the High Priest (Mark 14:53–65). Caiaphas asks Jesus if he is the Messiah, the Son of the most high God, and Jesus replies 'I am'.

Jesus/Saviour

- Jesus calms the storm (Mark 4:35–41). Jesus calms the storm with the words, 'Be still'. This shows that Jesus has God's authority and may represent for the persecuted Christians a means of escape from the Romans.

- The feeding of the five thousand (Mark 6:30–44). Jesus gives the people bread as Moses did. He is their saviour then and later when he gives his gift of himself in bread at the Last Supper. He offers a means of redemption (being saved) for all forever. He saves in a human and divine way.

- The Syro-Phoenician woman's daughter (Mark 7:24–30). Jesus has authority to heal from a distance and although he comes first for the Jews, he will also offer redemption to the Gentiles.

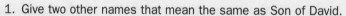

PROGRESS CHECK

1. Give two other names that mean the same as Son of David.
2. Give one reason why Jesus refers to himself as Son of Man.
3. Cite two occasions where Jesus is referred to as Son of God.
4. What person of Jesus is revealed at the feeding of the 5000?
5. Why is the term Son of Man important to readers of Mark's Gospel?
6. Cite three occasions when Jesus is called Christ/Messiah or Son of David.

1. Messiah, Christ. 2. He wants to keep the fact that he is the Messiah secret (Messianic Secret), or he is indicating his humanity', or his other names were considered blasphemous. 3. At his Baptism and at the transfiguration. 4. Saviour. 5. It reveals Jesus' humanity. 6. Caesarea Philippi, Healing of Blind Bartimaeus and the triumphal entry into Jerusalem.

2.2 *The importance of the Gospels*

After studying this section you should:

- *know why the Gospels were written*
- *know the different interpretations of the Gospels*
- *understand how the Gospels were spread*
- *know the key groups in Jesus' lifetime and the environment he worked in*
- *understand how the Gospels are important to Christians today*

 The Gospels are your most important resource in a study of Christianity. Christians obtain most of their knowledge and understanding of Jesus from the Gospels.

Christians regard the Gospels as the **Word of God** and often treat them with more awe and reverence than other parts of the Bible.

Gospel

- Gospel means 'good news'. It comes from the Greek word **evanglion**; hence the Gospel writers are called **evangelists** because they are proclaiming the Good News: the Good News that Jesus is the Messiah and came to show people a new way of living.

- The bulk of the Gospel texts are concerned with the last three years of Jesus' life, when he was teaching, and they also give much space to a description of his arrest, trial, death and resurrection.

The Synoptic Gospels

- The Gospels of Mark, Luke and Matthew are called the Synoptic Gospels because they are all similar to one another, containing much information that is common to all three.

- Mark was written first, but Matthew and Luke share information not contained in Mark; this information is believed to have come from a source now lost but known as Q.

- Similarly, information that is unique to Matthew or Luke is respectively referred to as arising from sources known as M and L.

The context in which Jesus lived

- The geography of Palestine has not changed. It contains both desert and fertile areas.
- The people at the time were mainly farmers and manual workers, keeping sheep or providing simple services like carpentry and pottery.
- Palestine was occupied by the Romans and was multi-racial, with many languages and cultures.
- Jesus was born a Jew and therefore is identified with that culture.
- When Jesus began his ministry he came into contact with the influential people of Palestine and of his own community. The Gospels show how conflict arose between them because he was declaring a completely new and radical way of looking at life.

Key Gospel groups

Pharisees	In the Gospels, they are shown by Jesus to be Jews who put the letter of the law above the needs of men. They were completely committed to observance of the oral law and the Torah but also accepted the Prophets and writings as Scripture. Jesus often challenges them and calls them hypocrites.
Sadducees	A politically influential group who recognised only the Torah as law and colluded in compromising with the Roman authorities to keep their influence.
The Sanhedrin	The Jewish Council which decided religious matters. It had 70 members and was presided over by the high priests.
Herodians	Supporters of Herod the Great. Mainly wealthy Jews who wanted a nationalist party.
Zealots	Jews who wanted to overthrow Roman rule by terrorism.
Tax collectors	Jewish employees of Rome regarded as outcasts by the rabbis.
Samaritans	A race of people living between Judea and Galilee who accepted the Torah but were not regarded as Jews and were much despised.

The Synagogue was the place of worship for the Jewish community and the Sabbath was the Holy Day.

 KEY POINT

Some Christians interpret the Gospel literally. They are 'fundamentalists' who accept every word as it is written. Others interpret the Gospel liberally, which means more freely, accepting that although the basic facts never change, some interpretations change with society.

Mark's Gospel

AQA A   AQA C
EDEXCEL A   EDEXCEL B
OCR A
WJEC
NICCEA

The Lion is the symbol of Mark's Gospel. It represented strength and courage to the early Christians and disciples.

- Mark's Gospel is ascribed to a certain Mark, or John. Although it is not certain who wrote it, it is accepted that this Gospel was written in about AD 60 in Rome.
- It is likely that Mark got his information from Peter.

Mark wrote his Gospel because:

- key people who knew Jesus and remembered the stories were dying
- the stories needed to be preserved
- persecuted Christians needed strength from Jesus' life
- it was important to have a written record of the events of Jesus' life

There are good reasons to believe that Mark's Gospel is written for a non-Jewish readership:

- Words are translated from Aramaic.
- There is strong emphasis on the suffering of Jesus and on the necessary acceptance of possible suffering on the part of the disciples.

Mark's Gospel was spread by:

- word of mouth
- people living by the teachings of Jesus

Interpreting the Gospel

AQA A   AQA C
EDEXCEL A   EDEXCEL B
OCR A
WJEC
NICCEA

Literalist	Some people interpret every word in the Gospel as literally true. Hence there are some groups in America who pick up venomous snakes during their services and drink poison (Mark 16:18).
Fundamentalist	Some people believe the Gospel to be the Word of God. Events happened just as they are written to show that Jesus is God.
Conservative	A conservative interpretation is one where the reader considers carefully the context in which the Gospel is written and takes account of different versions of miracles.
Liberals	Other people interpret the Bible as a more flexible way of exploring the message of God. Liberals believe the stories represent God's love for humanity through the person Jesus.

PROGRESS CHECK

1. Why did Mark write his Gospel?
2. How was Mark's Gospel spread?
3. Name four different interpretations of the Bible.
4. Who were the Pharisees?
5. What was the Sanhedrin?

1. To have a written record; to record what happened before eye-witnesses died; to give courage to persecuted Christians; to explain things for the Gentiles; to proclaim the Good News. 2. By word of mouth. 3. Literalist, fundamentalist, conservative, liberalist. 4. The Pharisees were ultra-strict Jews who believed themselves to be above other Jews. They did not mix with others. 5. The Sanhedrin was the Jewish Council presided over by the High Priests.

2.3 *Miracles in Mark*

LEARNING SUMMARY

After studying this section you should:

● **know the different types of miracle performed by Jesus**
● **understand the purpose of the miracle accounts**
● **know the connection between faith and prayer and miracles**
● **know the key events of the miracles in Mark's Gospel**

Meaning of miracles

AQA A   AQA C
EDEXCEL A   EDEXCEL B
OCR A
WJEC
NICCEA

● In Mark's Gospel, Jesus performs many different types of miracle to demonstrate the nature of Jesus.

● Jesus performs miracles to show that he has God's power over nature and physical and mental illness.

● He also shows that it is necessary to have faith in order for a miracle to happen.

● The occurrence of miracles does not lead to faith.

- It does not matter whether Christians believe the miracles really happened in a supernatural sense.

KEY POINT

> A miracle is simply an event that is not explicable in a normal way.

- Today, some scientists say there is a logical explanation for every miracle, but most believers do not search for a reason.

- The miracle accounts, and what Jesus teaches about faith, are part of the Gospel writer's Good News. They tell the reader about the person Jesus.

KEY POINT

> Miracles can be thought of in three dimensions:
>
> **Terras** is the awe and wonder, the amazement, with which onlookers regarded miracles.
> **Dynamis** is the power that was displayed.
> **Semeion** is the meaning, which may be apparent to the healed and those witnessing the event.

Nature miracles

Jesus calms the storm (Mark 4:35–41)

When Jesus calms the storm he says to his frightened disciples, '**Have you no faith?**' Then they ask one another who he can be; they are with awe (terras) at the power (dynamis) of Jesus and they wonder what it can mean (semeion).

That day, in the evening, he said to them, 'Let us cross over to the other side of the lake'. So they left the crowd and took him with them in the boat where he had been sitting; and there were other boats accompanying him. A heavy squall came on and the waves broke over the boat until it was all but swamped. Now he was in the stern, asleep on a cushion.
They roused him and said, 'Master we are sinking! Do you not care?' He awoke, rebuked the wind and said to the sea, 'Hush be still!' The wind dropped and there was dead calm. He said to them, 'Why are you such cowards? **Have you no faith even now?**' They were awestruck and said to one another, 'Who can this be? Even the wind and the sea obey him.'

Jesus feeds five thousand (Mark 6:30–44)

- When Jesus has a large crowd to feed, he gathers five loaves and two fish.

- He looks up to heaven and gives thanks to God. Then he breaks the bread.

- When the disciples distribute it to the crowd, there is enough for all of them with twelve baskets of leftovers.

KEY POINT

> Jesus is always recognised by Christians in the breaking of bread. He is the source of all life for them.

Jesus walks on water (Mark 6:45–52)

- Jesus comes to the disciples in their boat by walking on the water and they are terrified, thinking he is a ghost.

- He calms them, but they are amazed because, despite the feeding of the five thousand, they still do not understand his power.

> The water is symbolic of chaos, evil and darkness. Jesus shows his power over these things. Water is also a symbol of new life and is constantly referred to in the Bible. Walking on water shows power, like the power God demonstrates in the parting of the Red Sea (Exod. 14).

In Mark 8:1–9, Jesus again feeds a large crowd; this time there are four thousand people. Jesus uses the same method but only seven loaves. Again there are seven baskets of leftovers.

Miracles of healing – mental illness

 KEY POINT — Jesus is seen to heal many people who are possessed by evil spirits. They seem to have symptoms that might today be regarded as those of mental illness.

A man with an evil spirit (Mark 1:21–28)

Jesus is preaching in the synagogue on the Sabbath when a man with an evil spirit says to him, 'What do you want with us Jesus of Nazareth? Are you here to destroy us? I know who you are, you are God's holy messenger!'
Jesus replies, 'Be quiet and come out of that man.'
The evil spirit shook the man hard, gave a loud scream and came out of him.
The people in the synagogue were **amazed** and questioned Jesus' **authority**.

A man with evil spirits (The Gerasene Demoniac) (Mark 5:1–20)

This man lived in the territory of Gerasa and was possessed by so many evil spirits that his feet and hands had been chained. He smashed the chains and roamed the hills, screaming and cutting himself with stones.
When he sees Jesus he calls him **the Son of the most high God** and begs him not to punish him. Jesus is quietly ordering the evil out of the man.
Jesus asks, 'What is your name?' and the man replies, 'Mob, there are so many of us.'
Jesus sends the spirits from Mob into the pigs feeding nearby and they all rush over the cliff into the lake and drown.
After this, Mob is sensible and quiet. He wants to go with Jesus but Jesus orders him to go through the ten towns telling people what Jesus has done for him.

The Syro-Phoenician woman's daughter (Mark 7:24–30)

It is important in Mark that Jesus heals all people, including Gentiles, and the Jewish term for dog was used for Gentiles. The woman had absolute faith that Jesus would heal her daughter and did not rush him.

This woman came to Jesus and told him her daughter had an evil spirit. She begged Jesus to drive out the demon and Jesus said, 'Let us first feed the children.'
The woman, who was a Gentile, agreed saying that even the dogs could eat the scraps later. Jesus told her that because of her answer she would find her daughter cured when she returned home, as indeed she did.

The boy with the evil spirit (Mark 9:14–29)

This is an important story, illustrating the **importance of faith in the working of miracles**.

- A boy has fits and the disciples cannot cure him. (These fits are described as similar to epilepsy.)

- Jesus chastises the disciples for their lack of faith and asks for the boy to be brought to him.

- The 'spirit' throws the boy on the floor and Jesus tells the boy's father that his son can be healed if only the father has faith.

- The father says he has faith, but begs for more. **'I have faith,'** cried the boy's father, **'Help me where faith falls short.'**
- Jesus then heals the boy, and, in reply to the disciples' questions, says that only prayer can drive out demons of this sort.

> **KEY POINT** It is important to search for faith and to pray for faith, rather than to pray for miracles.

Miracles of healing – physical illness

Jesus heals many people (Simon's mother-in-law) (Mark 1:29–34). Jesus very quietly heals Simon's mother-in-law of a fever and then goes on to heal many who are brought to him when the Sabbath is ended.

Jesus heals a man with a dreaded skin disease (Mark 1:40–45)

This miracle shows the faith of the man and Jesus emerging as a public figure.

A man approaches Jesus and says, 'If you want to, you can make me clean.' Jesus says he wants to, and cures the man, saying, 'Be clean.' He tells the man to keep the healing a secret but the man tells many people, thus increasing Jesus' fame and notoriety.

Jesus heals a paralysed man (Mark 2:1–12)

- Jesus is surrounded in a house and some men bring their friend to be cured.
- When they cannot reach Jesus they lower the man through the roof on his mat.
- Jesus tells the man his sins are forgiven and some in the crowd are astonished, saying, **'It is blasphemy as only God can forgive sins.'**
- Jesus asks which is easier, to forgive sins or cure the man.
- Then he tells the man to pick up his mat and walk. The man does so.
- **Jesus says, 'I will prove to you that the Son of Man has authority on earth to forgive sins.'**

Jesus calls himself the Son of Man and shows He has God's power not only to heal but to forgive as well.

The man with the paralysed hand (Mark 3:1–6)

- A man with a paralysed hand is in the synagogue on the Sabbath and Jesus calls him up and asks, 'What does our law allow us to do on the Sabbath? To help or to harm? To save a man's life or to destroy it?'
- Jesus heals the man and we are told that some Herodians met with some Pharisees to plot to kill Jesus.
- It is an important part of Jesus' developing ministry that he challenges the Pharasaical application of the Sabbath laws. When he makes this challenge by performing spectacular miracles it is very threatening to the authorities.

Jesus heals the haemorrhagic (Mark 5:25–34)

- A woman touches Jesus' cloak because she believes in doing so she can be cured of the bleeding which has afflicted her for years. She is healed and Jesus feels the power leave him.
- He asks who touched him, and when the woman comes forward he tells her that her **faith has cured her**.

Mark shows that people do not need to ask for healing – they only need faith.

Jairus' daughter (Mark 5:21–42)

- Jairus begs Jesus to heal his daughter by laying his hands on her but then a messenger comes to say the girl is dead.
- Jesus goes with Peter, James and John to Jairus' house saying, 'Don't be afraid; only believe.'
- When he arrives he asks why everyone is weeping and wailing.
- He says the child is not dead, only sleeping.
- He takes the child's parents and his own companions in with him.
- He goes to her and, taking her hand, tells her to 'get up little girl' ('Talitha Koum').
- She gets up and walks around.
- Everyone is beside themselves with amazement.
- He then says she should be given something to eat.
- He gives strict orders that no one should be told what has happened.

> Mark quotes the original Aramaic 'Talitha Koum', which Jesus might have used, to make the episode authentic to his readers.

> Candidates need to learn the sequence of events in this miracle as they occur exactly.

Jesus heals a deaf mute (Mark 7:31–37)

- A deaf mute is brought to Jesus by his friends and Jesus heals him in a very physical way.
- Jesus puts his fingers in the man's ears, spits and touches the man's tongue, saying, 'Ephphatha' (open up).
- Jesus does this away from the crowd and the man is cured.
- When the crowd sees what Jesus has done they are filled with **wonder**.

The blind man at Bethsaida (Mark 8:22–25)

- A blind man is also presented to Jesus by his friends.
- Jesus leads the man from the village, spits on his eyes and also touches his eyes until he can see clearly.
- The man is asked not to return to the village.

It is not clear why Jesus orders secrecy. It is possible he does not want to draw too much attention to himself yet or appear too threatening. Performing miracles is not his major task; it is part of his ministry to the sick.

Fig. 2.1 Jesus healing the blind man

PROGRESS CHECK

1. What is the connection between miracles and faith?
2. Name three levels on which miracles can be considered.
3. What kinds of miracles did Jesus perform?
4. What did miracles reveal about Jesus?
5. Name one miracle when Jesus raised someone from the dead.
6. How did Jesus heal the Gerasene Demoniac?
7. Why could the disciples not heal the boy with an evil spirit?
8. Why was the haemorrhagic woman healed?
9. Why does Jesus say, 'Your sins are forgiven' when he cures a paralysed man?
10. Why does Jesus order secrecy when he has cured someone?

1. It is necessary to have faith for miracles to occur. 2. Terras, dynamis and semeion, meaning wonder/awe, power. 3. Miracles of healing physical and mental illness, nature miracles and raising from the dead. 4. Miracles revealed that Jesus had God's power. 5. He raised Jairus' daughter. 6. Jesus sent the evil spirits from the Gerasene Demoniac into the pigs. 7. The disciples could not heal the boy with an evil spirit because they did not pray properly for faith. 8. The haemorrhagic woman was healed because she believed she only had to touch Jesus to be healed. She had faith. 9. Jesus has God's power to forgive sins and therefore to heal people. 10. Jesus orders secrecy because it is not time to reveal the Messianic Secret.

2.4 The parables of the Kingdom of God

LEARNING SUMMARY

After studying this section you should:

● **know what the Kingdom of God means to Christians**
● **understand why Jesus told parables**
● **know the sequence of events in the parables told by Jesus**
● **be able to explain what the parables meant to Christians then and what they mean now**

> Different Christians have different understandings of what is meant by the Kingdom of God.

KEY POINT

The Kingdom of God can be heaven or eternal life with God. The Kingdom of God can also be realised on earth when all things come under God's rule; all people live according to Jesus' teaching. The Kingdom of God may be realised when Jesus comes again to judge all people (Second Coming).

What is a parable?

AQA A   AQA C
EDEXCEL A   EDEXCEL B
OCR A
WJEC
NICCEA

● A parable is usually a simple story with a clear and simple meaning.

● Jesus used the medium of parables because storytelling was part of the Palestinian culture.

● He utilises the imagery of farming and shepherding because those are the contexts that were familiar to his listeners.

● Sometimes the parables are quick and simple messages and at other times they are turned into allegories, each part representing something different.

A growing seed (Mark 4:26–29)

- A seed is planted and grows in good, fertile soil when the farmer sleeps.
- When it is fully developed the farmer harvests it.
- So too the Kingdom of God grows silently, waiting for the harvest.

A mustard seed (Mark 4:30–34).

- The mustard seed is the smallest of seeds, which grows into a huge plant with large branches to shelter birds.
- So the Kingdom of God grows and is a haven, a resting place for all who wish to shelter in it.

> **KEY POINT**
>
> **The new way**
> **Through the teachings in the parables, Jesus emphasises the fact that his way is a new way.**

The patches and the wineskins (Mark 2:18–22).

- This is one of the parables Jesus told that challenged the Pharisees.
- He tells them no one would use new cloth to patch an old coat as the new cloth would tear the old; and no one would put new wine into old skins as the skins would swell and burst.
- New wine must be poured into fresh skins.
- Jesus is clearly telling the Pharisees that his way is completely new. It is not an adaptation of old ways but a fresh and radical way of living.

Allegories in Mark

AQA A   AQA C
EDEXCEL A   EDEXCEL B
OCR A
WJEC
NICCEA

Candidates need to be totally familiar with this parable and especially with its meaning.

The parable of the sower (Mark 4:3–9; 13–20)

- In this parable Jesus likens the farmer sowing his seeds to someone sowing God's message.
- The seeds represent the Word of God.
- Seeds that fall on the path represent words that fall on willing ears but are quickly forgotten because of temptation, snatched away by Satan, just as seeds on the path are snatched away by birds.
- Seeds that fall on rocky ground take root and grow but die quickly. As the soil dries the roots die; and so sometimes the Word is rooted weakly and is lost in times of trouble and persecution.
- Seeds that fall among the weeds and thorns grow well until they are choked by other growth, just as the Word is choked by those who become worried about riches and things of the world.
- Seeds that fall on fertile soil grow and multiply to produce a rich harvest, just as words are heard by accepting people and the message is accepted and it multiplies.

Jesus is explaining the message to make clear that everyone should listen to the Word of God and allow nothing to detract from it, in order that the Kingdom can grow and flourish in each person.

The parable of the tenants in the vineyard (Mark 12:1–12)

- This parable is to be found in Chapter 12, whereas the others are in the early part of the Gospel. It is quite different in meaning and speaks of Jesus' purpose on earth. It has been turned into an allegory, with each part representing something about the life of Jesus.

- A man plants a vineyard and leaves it in the hands of tenants.

- When he sends servants to collect the profits they are beaten, so he finally sends his son. The tenants decide to kill the son, believing that the vineyard will then be theirs.

- The owner returns, throws out the tenants and hands the vineyard to others.

- **Jesus concludes that the stone the builders rejected was the most important stone. Once again the reader is told that the Pharisees plotted to kill Jesus because he told this parable against them.**

In this parable:

- **the vineyard represents Israel**
- **the tenants represent the Jews**
- **the servants represent the prophets**
- **the Son represents Jesus**
- **the owner represents God**

The teaching of Jesus through the parables was controversial and challenging; uncompromising in its rejection of the way of the Pharisees. Jesus knew that he was making enemies but he did not flinch from his dangerous path and radical message.

The messages of the parables can be used to demonstrate Christian inspiration working for the true meaning in the Gospels. Jesus was more concerned about people and their understanding of the Kingdom and he came with a simple, clear message.

PROGRESS CHECK

1. What is a parable?
2. What is an allegory?
3. What is the Kingdom of God?
4. Name one parable in Mark that is an allegory.
5. Why is the Kingdom of God like a mustard seed?
6. What sorts of people are represented by seed that is choked by weeds in the parable of the sower?
7. Why is it impossible to put new wine into old skins?
8. Who is the cornerstone that the builders rejected?

1. A parable is a story with a meaning. 2. An allegory is a story in which the elements all represent something else. 3. The Kingdom of God is heaven or it is earth when everyone lives according to God's law. 4. The parable of the sower or the tenants in the vineyard. 5. The Kingdom of God starts off small and then grows large like a mustard seed, providing branches for all kinds of people. 6. The seeds choked by weeds represent people who hear the word of God but give up on it when they become too engrossed in things of the world. 7. New wine in old skins will cause the skins to burst and Jesus' way is a new way, not a patching up of the old way. 8. Jesus.

2.5 Episodes of conflict

After studying this section you should:

● know the occasions when Jesus is in open conflict with the authorities
● understand the significance of the Sabbath laws of the time and their relevance to Christians today
● know the details of the episodes of conflict

KEY POINT   Jesus directly challenged the established authority, not only through his parables but also through direct action and teachings.

The Sabbath laws

AQA A   AQA C
EDEXCEL A   EDEXCEL B
OCR A
WJEC
NICCEA

● The Pharisees applied the Sabbath laws very rigidly.
● They had hundreds of sub-clauses about what constituted work on the Sabbath. No one was allowed to carry more ink than was necessary to write two letters or more oil than was necessary to anoint the nail of the smallest toe.
● Jesus cast these petty rules aside.

Picking corn on the Sabbath

● When the disciples pick ears of corn on the Sabbath they are accused of 'working'.
● Jesus responds by reminding the Pharisees that David and his men ate bread designated for the high priest on the Sabbath because they were hungry.
● He tells them the Sabbath is made for man, not man for the Sabbath (Mark 2:23–27). He says the same thing when he heals the man with the withered hand, showing that it is more important to do good on the Sabbath; to help not to destroy.

The man with the withered hand

On another occasion when Jesus went to the synagogue, there was a man in the congregation who had a withered arm; and they were watching to see whether Jesus would cure him on the Sabbath, so that they could bring a charge against him. He said to the man with the withered arm, 'Come and stand out here.' Then he turned to them: **'Is it permitted to do good or to do evil on the Sabbath, to save life or to kill?'** They had nothing to say and, looking round at them with anger and sorrow at their obstinate stupidity, he said to the man, 'Stretch out your arm.' He stretched it out and his arm was restored. But the Pharisees, on leaving the synagogue, began plotting against him with the partisans of Herod to see how they could make away with him. (Mark 3:1–6)

Ritual washing

AQA A AQA C
EDEXCEL A EDEXCEL B
OCR A
WJEC
NICCEA

Jesus challenges the Pharisees about their elaborate teaching on cleanliness. It was considered necessary to wash hands in a ritual way after they had touched anything that might make them unclean. Food from the market and other items had to be ritually washed.

Jesus chastises the Pharisees, saying they only apply the law when it suits them and treat their parents badly by declaring that all their goods are 'corban' (belonging to God) and cannot be used to help the elderly. Jesus says it is the things that come out of a person that make him unclean – immoral things such as murder, slander, adultery, jealousy, indecency, pride and deceit. What a person takes in physically does not make him unclean in a real sense as a person.

Paying taxes

AQA A AQA C
EDEXCEL A EDEXCEL B
OCR A
WJEC
NICCEA

- Some Pharisees and Herod's men try to trap Jesus by asking him who they should pay taxes to.
- Jesus shows them the Emperor's head on a coin and tells them to pay to the emperor what belongs to him and to God what belongs to God.
- Jesus has the measure of the Pharisees and is not afraid to confront them and outwit them, if necessary, to underline his message. He is not a revolutionary about to overthrow the government. He has come to challenge the distortions in following the way of God.

PROGRESS CHECK

1. Give two examples of the rigidity of the Sabbath laws at the time.
2. What did Jesus reply when his disciples were accused of picking corn on the Sabbath?
3. What, according to Jesus, makes someone unclean?
4. What does 'corban' mean?
5. What does Jesus mean when he says, 'Pay unto Caesar what belongs to Caesar and to God what belongs to God'?

1. Jews were not supposed to carry any more oil than needed to anoint a small toe or any more ink than necessary to write two letters. 2. Jesus reminded them that David's men had eaten the bread in the temple and said that the sabbath was made for man, not man for the sabbath; the Son of man is Lord even of the sabbath. 3. That which comes from within, evil thoughts, fornication, theft, murder, adultery, greed, slander, malice, fraud, indecency, envy, arrogance and folly. 4. Corban was a way of saying that something was set aside for God and could not be used therefore for the benefit of others. 5. Jesus is making it clear that he is not a political leader and the law must be obeyed, but that God has his law too. He would not fall into the trap of stating that people should not pay taxes to the occupying Roman forces.

2.6 Discipleship

 LEARNING SUMMARY

After studying this section you should:

● *know the most important aspect of Mark's Gospel is the message he conveys about what is necessary to be a follower of Jesus, i.e. to be a disciple*

● *know that it is from these passages that you can find much evidence to support Christian teachings on attitudes to contemporary moral issues*

The section on discipleship is mainly contained in Mark 8:22–10:52. It begins with the curing of the blind man at Bethsaida and ends with the curing of Blind Bartimaeus. These episodes can be seen as symbolic. Until people recognise the way of discipleship they are blind. Only when they understand the cost of being a follower of Jesus can they be considered to have seen the new way and become enlightened.

Leadership/Call of the disciples

AQA A   AQA C
EDEXCEL A   EDEXCEL B
OCR A
WJEC
NICCEA

When Jesus calls the disciples they drop everything and follow him without question (Mark 1:16–20). He said to Simon and Andrew, 'Come with me and I will make you fishers of men.'

He appointed the twelve: Simon (Peter); James and John (Boanerges); Andrew, Philip, Bartholomew, Matthew, Thomas, James, Thadeus, Simon and Judas Iscariot.

He gave the disciples their mission and sent them out.

● They went in pairs to have authority over unclean spirits.

● They were to take nothing except a stick.

● They took no bread, no pack and no money.

● They took only sandals, no extra coat.

● When admitted to a house they should stay until they left.

● When not welcome somewhere they should leave and shake the dust from their feet.

Jesus commissioned his disciples after his resurrection. He told them to:

'Go forth and proclaim the good news. Those who believe it will be saved; those who don't will be condemned. Believers will cast out demons in my name, speak in strange tongues, handle snakes or drink any deadly poison and come to no harm. They will lay hands on the sick and they will recover.' (Mark 16:15–18)

Peter's confession of faith (Caesarea Philippi)

AQA A   AQA C
EDEXCEL A   EDEXCEL B
OCR A
WJEC
NICCEA

> Peter loves Jesus and, although he recognises Jesus as the Messiah, he is not able to see what kind of Messiah Jesus is.

- Jesus asks the disciples 'Who do people say I am?'
- They tell him that some say John the Baptist, some say Elijah, others say one of the prophets.
- He asks, 'Who do you say I am?'
- Peter replies, 'You are the Messiah.'
- Then he gave them strict orders not to tell anyone about him and began to teach them that the Son of Man had to undergo great sufferings, to be rejected by the priests, doctors and teachers of the law; to die and rise again three days later.
- When Peter rebukes Jesus for this talk, Jesus says to him, 'Away Satan, you think as men think, not as God thinks.'

> **KEY POINT** Jesus' admonition to secrecy is known as the Messianic Secret. It must not yet be revealed that Jesus is the Messiah.

Taking up the cross

AQA A   AQA C
EDEXCEL A   EDEXCEL B
OCR A
WJEC
NICCEA

> **KEY POINT** The taking of the cross is the central theme of Mark's Gospel, and a message to the persecuted Christians in Rome.

- Jesus tells the crowd and his followers: 'If anyone wants to come with me, he must forget self, carry his cross and follow me. For whoever wants to save his own life will lose it; but whoever wants to lose his life for me and for the Gospel will save it. Does a person gain anything if he wins the whole world but loses his life? Of course not.' (Mark 8:34–36)
- Taking up the cross had a literal meaning for Mark's readers who faced death for their Christian beliefs. Even today, Christians in many areas are killed for their beliefs. Roman Catholic priests and nuns, for example, have been murdered in El Salvador because their work with the poor was seen as a threat to the government.
- This idea is reinforced when Peter, James and John witness the transfiguration of Jesus on the mountain (Mark 9:2–9) and see him with Moses and Elijah.
- Jesus tells them the Son of Man will suffer and die. The Scriptures will be fulfilled, just as they were when people treated Elijah as they pleased.

Qualities of a follower (disciple)

There are, then, certain passages that allow the reader to see the qualities that are necessary to be a follower of Jesus carrying the cross.

- **A follower must have faith** as the father of the boy with an evil spirit has faith and prays for more faith, believing anything is possible for those who have faith.
- **A follower must have humility.** Jesus says, 'Whoever wants to be first must place himself last of all and be the servant of all' (Mark 9:35).

- **A follower should love children.** Jesus says, 'Whoever welcomes in my name one of these children, welcomes me; whoever welcomes me, welcomes not only me but the one who has sent me' (Mark 9:37).

- **A follower is anyone who is for Jesus.** (Therefore Christians of any denomination) 'For whoever is not against us is for us' (Mark 9:40).

- **A follower must have fidelity in marriage.** Jesus says, 'Man must not separate what God has joined together' (Mark 10:9) and 'A man who divorces his wife and marries another woman commits adultery against his wife. In the same way, a woman who divorces her husband and marries another man commits adultery' (Mark 10:11–12).

Fig. 2.2 Jesus with children

This is a radical aspect of Jesus' teaching, which many Christians cite for working with the 'poorest of the poor' and living lives in poverty. (Mother Theresa)

- **A follower must receive the Kingdom of God like a child.** 'Let the children come to me and do not stop them for the Kingdom of God belongs to such as these. I assure you that whoever does not receive the Kingdom of God like a little child, will not enter it' (Mark 10:14–15). Children receive and believe in innocence, which is often lost through the trials of life. Adults have to struggle to hold onto a childlike faith.

- **A follower must sell all he has and give it to the poor.** When the rich young man asks Jesus what he must do to enter the Kingdom of Heaven, Jesus tells him to obey the commandments. He says he has done this since childhood so Jesus tells him he must sell everything, give it to the poor and follow Jesus. The rich man goes away sad because he is very rich and Jesus tells the disciples, 'It is much harder for a rich person to enter the Kingdom of God than for a camel to go through the eye of a needle' (Mark 10:17–21).

- **A follower must be servant of all.** When James and John ask if they can sit either side of Jesus on his glorious throne, he tells them they have no idea of the suffering he must endure. He tells them, 'If one of you wants to be great, he must be the servant of the rest' (Mark 10:43).

The rewards of discipleship

Those who give up everything to follow Jesus will receive a **hundred times** more fathers, mothers, brothers, sisters, land and persecutions as well as eternal life.

KEY POINT
These passages spell out clearly that Mark's message is that the Gospel values are difficult to hold on to; they are difficult ways to follow and Jesus sets a hard path for his would-be followers. Christianity is not a 'soft' way of life, but a very challenging way to live.

PROGRESS CHECK

1. List the qualities needed to be a disciple of Jesus.
2. What are the rewards of discipleship?
3. What must you do to be a disciple of Jesus?
4. What did Jesus say to the rich young man who wanted to enter the Kingdom of Heaven?
5. Name a modern Christian who lived like a true disciple of Jesus.
6. What was the mission of the disciples?
7. What was the commission of the disciples?

1. Faith, humility, love of children, being for Jesus, fidelity in marriage, receiving the Kingdom of God like a child. 2. The hundred-fold: a hundred times more brothers, sisters, mothers, fathers, land, persecutions and eternal life. 3. Take up your cross and follow. 4. He said he had to sell everything, give it to the poor and follow Jesus. 5. Mother Theresa of Calcutta. 6. The mission was to go out in pairs with sandals and a stick, with no extra coat, no bread, money or pack and cast out unclean spirits, staying where they were welcome and leaving when people would not listen. 7. The commission was to proclaim the Good News, baptise people, speak in strange tongues, handle snakes and drink deadly poison and take no harm, to heal people in Jesus' name.

The Passover meal

AQA A   AQA C
EDEXCEL A   EDEXCEL B
OCR A
WJEC
NICCEA

- Jesus is asked by his disciples where he wishes them to prepare the Passover meal. He instructs them to follow a man carrying a jar into a house and tells them that the owner of the house will lead them to an upper room.
- When they are all assembled in the upper room Jesus says one of them will betray him and they all deny it.
- Jesus tells them that the one who dips his bread with him will be the traitor and 'It would be better for that man if he had never been born' because he will betray the Son of Man.

The Lord's Supper

- During the meal Jesus breaks bread, says a prayer of thanks, and says, '**Take it, this is my body**'. (Mark 14:23)
- He gives the cup of wine, and says, '**This is my blood which is poured out for many, my blood which seals God's covenant**'. (Mark 14:24)
- He also predicts that Peter will deny him.

KEY POINT
> The Lord's Supper is the institution of the Eucharist and is the central part of much Christian worship. The remembrance of Christ and his sacrifice is commemorated at the breaking of bread by Christians together.

Fig. 2.3 The Last Supper

Candidates should be aware that Roman Catholic Christians believe in the doctrine of 'transubstantiation', that when Roman Catholic priests break bread in the Mass, Jesus becomes really present in substance. In the Protestant tradition, the minister re-enacts the Last Supper and Jesus becomes symbolically present to the worshippers.

Because of these differences in doctrine, the Roman Catholic Church forbids its members to participate in shared Communion with other denominations, except in exceptional circumstances.

The arrest, trial and death of Jesus

- In Mark's Gospel a great deal of emphasis is placed on Jesus' suffering and death.
- Mark wishes to convey the extent of the suffering of Jesus, his humiliation, the injustice of his situation, his own fear and the horrible pain of his crucifixion.

The Garden of Gethsemane

- When Jesus prayed in the Garden of Gethsemane, he asked his Father to take away his cup of suffering because he was deeply distressed by the fear of His coming death.
- Jesus nevertheless told his Father that he would do what his Father wanted him to do; not what he himself wanted (Mark 14:32–41).
- This passage shows what is expected of Christian disciples. They must be prepared to discern God's will and accept it, even if it means their own death.

Jesus is betrayed

- Jesus was arrested when Judas betrayed him by a kiss; this was a signal to the chief priests and the teachers of the law and the elders (Mark 14:43–52) to seize him in the garden.
- Jesus did not resist the arrest. He knew that his teaching and actions were seen as a threat to the authorities.

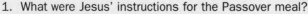

1. What were Jesus' instructions for the Passover meal?
2. What did Jesus say about the person who would betray him?
3. What did Jesus say when he broke the bread?
4. What did Jesus say when he offered the cup of wine to the disciples?
5. How is the offering of bread and wine interpreted by Christians?
6. What did Jesus foretell of Peter at the Last Supper?
7. What did Jesus ask in the Garden of Gethsemane?
8. Who betrayed Jesus?

PROGRESS CHECK

1. Two disciples were to go to the city and follow the man carrying a jar of water and, when he enters a house, ask for the room prepared for the disciples to eat the Passover meal. They found everything as he said. 2. It would be better for that person not to have been born. 3. 'Take this; this is my body.' 4. 'This is my blood, the blood of the new covenant, shed for you.' 5. As a memorial of Jesus and a way of his being ever present to all Christians. 6. That Peter would deny him three times before the cock crowed twice. 7. For his cup of suffering to be taken from him. 8. Judas Iscariot for thirty pieces of silver and with a kiss.

Trial before the Sanhedrin

- At his trial before the council of religious leaders (Mark 14:53–65) many witnesses told lies about what Jesus had said and contradicted one another.

- The High Priest finally asked Jesus whether he was the Messiah, and Jesus replied, **'I am, and you will all see the Son of Man seated on the right of the Almighty coming with the clouds of heaven'**.

- The Jewish leaders were very angry to hear these words because the words 'I am' were sacred – suggesting that Jesus was divine. **He was declared guilty of blasphemy**.

Peter's denial

- During the trial, Peter, the leader of the disciples, denied to a waiting crowd that he knew Jesus (Mark 14:66–72).

- He was afraid that he would also be arrested for being a follower of Jesus. After the cock had crowed twice Peter remembered that Jesus had told him that he would deny that he knew Jesus. Peter broke down and cried.

- Peter's story was an example to the followers of Jesus of a man, their leader, who had turned away from following Jesus, but then returned to following Jesus after Jesus had forgiven him.

Trial before Pilate

- The high priests had Jesus taken before Pilate. They had declared him guilty of blasphemy but had no power to condemn him to death.

- Only the governor had that power. The high priests had already spread rumours that Jesus had called himself the King of the Jews, and that was treason.

- Pilate asked him, **'Are you the king of the Jews?'** and Jesus replied, **'The words are yours.'**

- Jesus did not reply to any of the accusations made against him.

- Pilate decided to offer Jesus as one of the prisoners for release for the Passover alongside a murderer called Barabbas. The crowd called for Barabbas and when Pilate asked what he should do with the one they called the King of the Jews they called out, **'Crucify him!'**

- So Pilate (to satisfy the mob) had Jesus flogged and handed him over to be crucified (Mark 15:1–15).

The death of Jesus

- Jesus was mocked.
- The soldiers took him into the governor's headquarters.
- They put a purple robe on him and twisted some thorns into a crown for his head.
- They called him 'King of the Jews' and bowed down and spat on him.

- Jesus was helped by Simon from Cyrene as he carried his own cross to the place called Golgotha (the Place of a Skull) where he was to die.
- Jesus refused the drugged wine (vinegar) he was offered.
- He was fixed to the cross and his executioners cast lots for his clothes.
- He was crucified at 9 o'clock in the morning and a sign was put over him, which said, 'The King of the Jews'.
- Passers-by mocked him, telling him to save himself as he had saved others or to come down from the cross and save himself if he really had the power to rebuild the temple in days.
- At 3 o'clock the land was covered in darkness and Jesus cried out, '**Eloi, Eloi, lema sabachthani?' (My God, My God, why have you abandoned me?)**
- Then Jesus gave a loud cry and died and the curtain in the Temple was torn in two.
- The centurion looked on Jesus and said, 'Truly this man was the Son of God.'
- It is thought that Jesus may have been crying out in the agony of his humanity that God had abandoned Him. Some scholars say that Jesus was uttering the beginning of Psalm 22, which ends joyously. The temple curtain tearing can be seen to symbolise that through his death Jesus had allowed all men to enter the 'Holy of Holies', which was a special curtained-off area of the temple where only high priests could go. This would be constant with Mark's theme that Jesus was clearing a path for a new way of living. The centurion's comments confirm that for Mark, Jesus was very much the Son of God, as even one of his murderers realised.

The Resurrection

AQA A   AQA C
EDEXCEL A   EDEXCEL B
OCR A
WJEC
NICCEA

> Candidates must know the exact sequence of the events of the death of Jesus in precise detail.

> Candidates must know exactly who Jesus appeared to and in what circumstances.

- On the day after the Sabbath, **Mary Magdalene, Mary the mother of James and Salome** go to anoint the body, as is the custom.
- They find the stone rolled away and the body gone.
- A young man tells them to go and tell Peter and the disciples that Jesus has gone to Galilee ahead of them.
- The women run from the tomb in distress.
- Readers are told that Jesus appears to Mary Magdalene, to two disciples in the country and to eleven disciples when they are eating. He scolds them for their fear and orders them to go out and preach the Gospel, driving out demons and performing miracles in His name.
- Jesus is then taken up to heaven.

PROGRESS
CHECK

1. How did Jesus chastise those who arrested him?
2. What was the charge against Jesus before the Sanhedrin?
3. What was Jesus asked by the High Priest and what did he reply?
4. What did Pilate ask Jesus and what did Jesus reply?
5. What did the soldiers do to Jesus after his trial?
6. What happened to Jesus before he was crucified at Golgotha?
7. How did the crowd taunt Jesus?
8. What did Jesus cry out before he died and what does it mean?
9. What did the centurion say of Jesus?
10. To which groups did Jesus appear after his resurrection?

1. 'Do you take me for a bandit that you have come with swords and cudgels to arrest me? Day after day I was within your reach as I taught in the Temple and you did not lay hands on me. But let the scriptures be fulfilled.' 2. Blasphemy. 3. 'Are you the Messiah, the Son of the blessed One?' 'I am and you will see the Son of Man seated at the right hand of God and coming with the clouds of heaven.' 4. 'Are you the King of the Jews?' 'The words are yours.' 5. Dressed him in purple robes, placed a crown of plaited thorns on his head, saluted him, 'Hail King of the Jews', beat him, spat on him, knelt in mock homage, then stripped him and dressed him again in his own clothes. 6. He was offered drugged wine, fastened to a cross, they cast lots for his clothes, nailed a sign on the cross 'The King of the Jews.' 7. 'You would pull down the Temple and build it in three days, come down from the cross and save yourself. If we see that, we shall believe.' 8. Eloi, Eloi, lema sabachthani (My God, My God, why have you abandoned me?) 9. 'Truly, this man was the Son of God.' 10. Mary Magdalene, two disciples walking on their way to the country, the eleven at table.

2.7 Luke's Gospel

LEARNING
SUMMARY

After studying this section you should know:

● the key events of Jesus' life as told by Luke
● Jesus' miracles in Luke
● Jesus' message about discipleship in Luke
● the institution of the Eucharist in Luke

Gospel events from Luke

AQA A | AQA C
EDEXCEL A | EDEXCEL B
OCR A
WJEC
NICCEA

KEY POINT

Candidates must study the section on Mark in conjunction with the section on Luke. The Mark section has the basic details; the differences in Luke are given here.

Luke was a Gentile and wrote his Gospel in a way that emphasised that Jesus was the saviour of all, Jews and Gentiles alike. It seems that Luke travelled with Paul and spoke to many people who had known Jesus although he had not known him. It is believed the Gospel was written in Rome in about AD 80–90.

The Infancy Narrative

● An old man called Zechariah is promised by the Angel Gabriel that his wife Elizabeth will have a child whom she will name John.

● Zechariah is struck dumb until the birth because he has difficulty believing what the angel has to say (Luke 1:11–20). Elizabeth had been thought to be barren (unable to bear children).

The Annunciation

- The Angel Gabriel visits the Virgin Mary and tells her she will conceive a son and give him the name Jesus.

- Mary is deeply troubled, but the angel tells her not to be afraid and says he will be called 'Son of the Most High'.

- Mary asks, 'How can this be, I am still a virgin?'

- She is told the Holy Spirit will come upon her and the child will be called 'Son of God'.

- Mary says, 'Here am I. I am the Lord's servant; as you have spoken so be it' (Luke 1:26–38).

> It is very important in Christian understanding that a young, vulnerable virginal girl accepted what she believed to be the will of the Lord in such a trusting way, despite the fear and uncertainty that the pregnancy would bring to her.

The Visitation

- Mary visits Elizabeth and Elizabeth's child moves in her womb.

- Elizabeth says, 'Who am I that the mother of my Lord should visit me?' and 'How happy is she who has had faith that the Lord's promise would be fulfilled.'

- Luke then writes the 'Magnificat' (Luke 1:46–56), which is Mary's song of praise for the work of the Lord and is an important prayer and a hymn of praise for Christians. It is used more often in Roman Catholic worship.

- The birth of John the Baptist. Elizabeth's son is a boy and Zechariah's speech returns and he praises the Lord in prophecy (Luke 1:68–79).

> Remember to link these episodes with questions on the celebration of Christian festivals.

The Nativity

- Luke tells how Mary and Joseph have to travel to Bethlehem for the census, which has been ordered by Caesar Augustus. (Luke is noted for his historical accuracy as a census did take place at about this time.)

- Mary gave birth to Jesus, wrapped him in swaddling clothes and laid him in a manger because there was no room for them to lodge in the inn (Luke 2:6–7).

The shepherds

- Some shepherds are visited by angels who tell them a Messiah has been born and he is in a manger.

- The shepherds hurry to Bethlehem to see the baby and tell Mary and Joseph what they have been told.

- Mary stores up this news in her heart while other listeners are astonished (Luke 2:8–19).

The presentation of Jesus

- Jesus is taken to be circumcised on the eighth day according to Jewish custom.

- Simeon visits him at the Temple.

- Simeon has been told by the Holy Spirit that he will not die until he has seen the Messiah.

- Simeon tells Mary that the child is destined to be a sign rejected by men and that Mary herself will be pierced to the heart.

- A woman, Anna, who prays every day in the Temple, tells Mary and Joseph that the child is the one to whom all are looking for the liberation of Jerusalem.

Jesus in the temple

- When Jesus is twelve years old, Mary and Joseph make a pilgrimage to Jerusalem. After they have left the city they cannot find Jesus and have to return.

- Eventually they find him teaching in the temple, talking and answering questions.

- When Mary chastises him, Jesus answers that she should expect to find him in his Father's house (Luke 2:41–50).

 KEY POINT Luke is very clear from the start that Jesus is the Messiah, the Son of God, the Son of the Most High, and that Mary treasures her knowledge about Jesus.

John the Baptist

- Luke gives more emphasis to John the Baptist than Mark. Both Gospel writers tell how John says he baptises with water but that the one who will come after him will baptise with the Holy Spirit.

- John also warns people to share their shirts and food, and live good lives.

- John baptises Jesus and the Spirit descends on him in the form of a dove. A voice from heaven is heard, saying, 'Thou art my Son, my Beloved, on thee my favour rests' (Luke 3:21,22; also Mark 1:10,11).

The temptations of Jesus (Luke 4:1–13)

- Luke tells his readers about the temptations.

- The devil tempts Jesus to turn stone to bread, but Jesus replies, 'Scripture says, "Man cannot live on bread alone."'

- The devil tempts Jesus to become master of all the Kingdoms of the world by doing homage to him (the devil), but Jesus tells him, 'Scripture says, "You shall do homage to the Lord your God and worship him alone."'

- The devil tempts Jesus to throw himself off the parapet of the temple and the angels of God will save him, but Jesus replies, 'It has been said, "You shall not put the Lord your God to the test."'

Christians recall the temptations and the wilderness during a time of fasting and abstinence in Lent. At this time they pray and reflect, trying to make spiritual ideas the focus of life and grow closer to Christ.

 PROGRESS CHECK

1. How does Elizabeth know that Mary is expecting a child?
2. What is Mary's response to the news that she has been chosen to be the mother of God?
3. What does Luke say that Mary does about the visit of the shepherds?
4. Who is the baby Jesus taken to see in the Temple?
5. What are the temptations of Jesus when he is in the desert?

1. When Mary greets Elizabeth, her own child leaps in her womb. 2. Mary is afraid but surrenders herself completely to the will of God. 3. Mary treasures all these things and ponders them in her heart. 4. Jesus is presented to Simeon who has waited many years to see the Messiah. 5. Turn stone to bread, pay homage to the devil and throw himself off a parapet to be saved by angels.

Miracles in Luke

 AQA A AQA C
EDEXCEL A EDEXCEL B
OCR A
WJEC
NICCEA

Those shown in bold are unique to Luke.

Mental illness

- The man with an evil spirit in the temple (Luke 4:31–37).
- Man at Gerasa (Gerasene Demoniac) (Luke 8:26–39).
- The epileptic boy (Luke 9:37–43).
- **Jesus heals a crippled woman** (Luke 1.3:10–17). A woman had been possessed by a spirit, which had caused her to be crippled for 18 years. When Jesus saw her he simply said, 'You are rid of your trouble' and the woman was cured. When he was criticised for doing this on the Sabbath he replied that the woman had been bound by Satan so it was appropriate to release her on the Sabbath.

Physical illness

- Simon's mother-in-law (Luke 4:38–39).
- Many people (Luke 4:40–41).
- A leper (Luke 4:12–16).
- The paralysed man (Luke 5:17–26).
- The man with the withered arm (Luke 6:6–11).
- **The centurion's servant** (Luke 7:1–10). A centurion's servant is ill so he sends some elders to ask Jesus to cure the servant. Jesus goes to the house but the centurion sends a message that he is not worthy to have Jesus in his house and asks Jesus only to cure the servant. Jesus admires the man's faith and the servant is cured.
- The haemorrhagic woman (Luke 8:43–48).
- Jairus' daughter (Luke 8:49–56).
- **A man with dropsy** (Luke 14:1–6). Jesus uses this episode to cure a man of dropsy on the Sabbath and at the same time challenge the Jewish Sabbath laws about work. He says to the Pharisees, 'Who among you would hesitate to haul his ox or ass to its feet if it fell on the Sabbath?'

- **The blind man of Jericho** (Luke 18:35–43). As Jesus passes by, the blind man calls out, 'Son of David, have pity on me!' and Jesus asks the man what he wants. The man replies that he wants his sight and Jesus cures him because of the faith he has shown. (This is the story of Bartimaeus given in Mark.)

- **The thankful leper** (Luke 17:11–19). Jesus cures ten lepers, telling them to go and show themselves to the priests. One, realising he is cured on the way to the priests, turns round and goes back to thank Jesus. Jesus tells him, 'Go, your faith has cured you.'

Nature miracles

- Jesus calms the storm (Luke 8:22–25).

- Jesus feeds the five thousand (Luke 9:10–17).

> **KEY POINT**
> The many miracles in Luke where Jesus cures Jews and Gentiles and especially outcasts teach that Jesus was especially concerned for the poorest, least exalted people in society.

Parables in Luke

AQA A   AQA C
EDEXCEL A   EDEXCEL B
OCR A
WJEC
NICCEA

Parables that are equivalent to those in Mark:

- The patches and the wineskins (Luke 5:36–39).

- The sower (Luke 8:4–8).

- The lamp under the bed – no one hides a lamp under a bed; it is put out for all to see (Luke 8:16–18).

- The mustard seed (Luke 13:18–19).

- The tenants in the vineyard (Luke 20:9–18).

Parables that do not appear in Mark and may be from Luke's source L or Q:

- **The Good Samaritan** (told in response to the question, 'Who is my neighbour?'; Luke 10:25–37). A man is attacked, beaten, robbed and left for dead. A priest and a Levite pass him by, but a Samaritan (regarded by the Jews as an enemy) stops, tends his wounds and takes the man to an inn, leaving money for him to be looked after until he has recovered. The neighbour is thus shown to be the one who showed the man kindness.

- **The rich fool** (Luke 12:13–21). A rich man grew many crops and decided to store them in a barn and then take life easy; but that night God said to him, 'You fool, this very night you must surrender your life; you have made your money – who will get it now?' (This is how it is for a man who amasses wealth for himself but remains a pauper in the eyes of God.) Jesus teaches that God clothes even the lilies in the fields and how much more will he look after his little ones. 'Set your mind upon His Kingdom and all the rest will come to you as well.'

- **The watchful servants** (Luke 12:35–40). Jesus teaches that servants should be alert for the master can return at any time. He says if the Master comes and finds his servants ready he will seat them and wait on them. He reinforces his point by saying that if the householder had known about the burglar, he would not have left his house. (From this story Christians understand that death comes like a thief in the night, stealing up on the unprepared.) This is a message to the Jews who compare the coming of the Messiah to a banquet. Jesus says all must be careful of their power. A servant without a master must not be too severe on others. From he who has much, much will be expected. Thus rights bring responsibility (Luke 12:41–48).

- **The Great Feast** (Luke 14:7–24). A man prepares a feast (verse 16) and invites his friends; they do not come, pleading business, possessions and relationships as excuses. The man sends his servants to find the poor and the beggars to sit at his table. He says, 'Not one of those who were invited shall taste my banquet.' This parable is about the messianic banquet to which many are called and should respond.

- **The lost sheep** (Luke 15:1–7). A farmer loses one sheep and leaves the other 99 to search for it; on finding it he rejoices. There is more rejoicing in heaven over one repentant sinner than over 99 righteous people who do not need to repent. Jesus emphasises his call to sinners, the weak in every way, the outcasts of society.

- **The lost coin** (Luke 15:8–10). This parable has a message similar to that of the lost sheep (above).

- **The prodigal (lost) son** (Luke 15:11–32). A younger son asks for his inheritance, takes it and spends it having a good time and winning many friends. When he has no money he has no friends and gets a job tending pigs and eating their swill. He decides his father's servants are better off so he returns home. When his father sees him he kills the best calf and has a big party. The elder son, who has stayed at home, says, 'Why do you never have a party for me?' His father tells him, 'Everything I have is yours but how can I help welcoming my son who was lost and is found?' This parable teaches about the constant forgiveness of the Father, God's unconditional love.

Fig. 2.4 The lost sheep

- **The shrewd manager** (unjust steward) (Luke 16:1–17). The shrewd manager uses his master's debts to win friends for himself. Jesus teaches that money can be put to good purpose but that someone untrustworthy in small things is untrustworthy in great things. He also says you cannot serve God and money.

- **The rich man and Lazarus** (Luke 16:19–31). This is the story of a rich man who is separated from Abraham after his death. He sees Lazarus, once a beggar, sitting with Abraham at a feast in heaven. The rich man begs that Lazarus might bring him water, but Abraham tells him that no one can cross the chasm between heaven and Hades (hell). On earth the rich man had everything and Lazarus nothing – now it is for Lazarus to have consolation. The rich man asks that someone be sent to warn his brothers of what will befall them, but Abraham says, 'If they pay no heed to Moses and the prophets, they will pay no heed to someone who rises from the dead.'

> Candidates should be able to transfer the teaching of the lost sheep to their understanding of what justification a Christian might give for working with a caring agency such as 'Shelter' or 'Crisis at Christmas'.

● **The gold coins** (Luke 19:11–27). A master goes away giving each of his ten servants one pound to trade with. One of them makes ten pounds from one, another makes five pounds, while a third makes none and only has the one pound to return to his master. His pound is taken from him to be given to the one with ten, and the master says, 'The man who has will be given more and the man who has nothing, even what he has will be taken from him.'

This difficult teaching is part of the justification for 'liberation theology', the means of using the teachings of Jesus to work for justice for the poor in the developing world especially.

KEY POINT

The purpose of the parables in Luke is to demonstrate Jesus' commitment to the poorest of the poor, to the outcasts, to sinners and the marginalised in society. They emphasise that Jesus was the Saviour of all.

PROGRESS CHECK

1. Which two people pass by without helping in the parable of the Good Samaritan?
2. Why does Jesus tell this story?
3. Why is the man who stores up riches on earth foolish?
4. Why should servants be watchful and how does this apply to Christians?
5. What is the point of the parable of the Great Feast?
6. Why is the elder brother jealous of the younger in the parable of the Lost (Prodigal) Son?
7. What does the rich man ask of Lazarus?
8. What does Lazarus say in response to his request?

1. The priest and the Levite. 2. To explain to his listeners who is your neighbour and to demonstrate that neighbours included everybody, even races or people that you might hate. 3. Because the rich fool might have to give up his life that night and he has amassed a fortune but is a pauper in the eyes of God. 4. The servants should be watchful because their master may return at any minute and Christians should be prepared because they never know when Christ will return to call them to himself. 5. That God will call to himself those who accept his invitation and act on it and will reject those who reject his invitation to be with him. 6. The father throws a feast for the younger brother who returns after wasting all his money and the elder brother has never had a feast although he has been with the father all the time. 7. That Lazarus should bring him water and warn his brother what might happen to them. 8. Lazarus says if they pay no heed to the prophets, they will not listen to him.

Discipleship in Luke

Much of Luke's Gospel indicates what is necessary for true disciples of Jesus. It is important to be humble, giving of self, forgiving of others, and to spend time with the poor and outcasts of society.

Jesus sends out twelve disciples (Luke 9:1–6). The disciples were told to go out and spread the Good News, heal people and drive out demons. (As Mark.)

In Luke's Gospel the following qualities are seen to be necessary in a disciple:

● To be prepared to take up the **cross day after day** (Luke 9:23–27).

● To be prepared for **homelessness** (Luke 9:58).

● To be prepared even to **put aside family responsibilities** (unlike the man who wants to bury his dead father, Luke 9:59,60).

● Not always to **look back to the family**. (Jesus fears that the man who wants to say goodbye to his family will be persuaded to change his mind, Luke 9:61,62)

● Not to stop or be deterred from a task (Jesus sends out the 72, Luke 10:1–24).

- To put **listening to the Word of God** before all things (Mary listens to Jesus while Martha fusses and works, Luke 10:38–42).

- To consider the implications of being a disciple carefully. As an owner counts the cost of constructing a tower over his vineyard, and a soldier weighs up the implications of mustering his armies, so must a would-be disciple make sure he is prepared to give with total commitment (Luke 14:25–33).

- **To sell all and give it to the poor** (Luke 18:18–30 as Mark 10:17–31).

- Being prepared to **give willingly**, as in the case of Zacchaeus (Luke 19:1–10).

- Being a **servant of all**, including children (Luke 9:46–48).

- Always being **prepared to forgive** – even up to seventy times seven (Luke 17:1–4).

- To **pray as Jesus taught** (Luke 11:1–13).

Fig. 2.5 Being a servant of all, including children

Episodes of conflict

AQA A   AQA C
EDEXCEL A   EDEXCEL B
OCR A
WJEC
NICCEA

Luke does not put too much emphasis on conflict between Jesus and the Jewish leaders or between Jesus and the Roman authorities since he is anxious to show that Jesus had a message for all people. He does, however, include conflict over the Sabbath.

- Disciples picking corn on the Sabbath (Luke 6:1–5).

- Healing the man with the withered arm (Luke 6:6–11).

- Jesus and Beelzebub (Luke 11:14–20).

- The parable of the mustard seed and the yeast (13:18–21).

Stewardship in Luke

AQA A   AQA C
EDEXCEL A   EDEXCEL B
OCR A
WJEC
NICCEA

Stewardship of possessions is emphasised in Luke. Jesus' parables in Luke have particular relevance to life in the late 20th century. People are aware today of a world stripped of its natural resources, and many are also aware of the futility and worthlessness of material possessions.

> The stewardship aspect of gospel teaching is important for understanding Christian attitudes to the environment.

- A man who is ready to sit back and enjoy the fortune he has amassed but could die that very night (Luke 12:13–21).

- A steward who misuses the assets of his master (Luke 16:19–31). (People are misusing the assets God gave them when he created man to have dominion over the earth.)

- The parable of the rich young man (Luke 18:18–30) is another warning of the foolishness of treasuring the things of the world.

- The parable of the servants with the master's coins (Luke 19:11–27) teaches them to care for gifts that have been given and use them wisely. In the same way, Christians believe man is cautioned to use the earth and its resources wisely.

The Lord's Supper

- Luke writes of Jesus instituting the Eucharist after giving out the cup of Passover. Luke adds a teaching from Jesus to his disciples about humble service leading to reward (22:24–30), which is a favourite theme for Luke.
- Luke also adds to Mark's account of Peter's denial of Jesus by saying that Peter would have a leadership role (Luke 22:3).
- Luke also adds a message from Jesus to the disciples that each must carry a sword on missionary work as they will be considered outlaws. This is a hint that their lives will be difficult and they might face death because of their work (Luke 22:35–38).
- Christians see in this passage a call from God to follow Jesus' way and accept the difficulties that come their way as a result.

The arrest, trial and death of Jesus

As in Mark's Gospel, Luke shows that the religious leaders were plotting against Jesus who prophesied he would suffer and be crucified by them.

The Garden of Gethsemane
Luke's version is shorter than Mark's account, but includes an angel (Luke 22:43). Luke includes angels in the infancy narratives also.

Jesus is betrayed
Luke adds to Mark's account the detail that the temple guards were among those who arrested Jesus and that Jesus healed the slave's ear after it was cut off by a disciple.
Luke also adds the idea that this was a time of darkness. Luke has already mentioned that Judas was under Satan's influence (Luke 22:3).

Trial before the Sanhedrin
Luke's account is similar to that in Mark but the trial is held in the morning. The witnesses who contradict one another, mentioned in Mark, are missed out in Luke. Luke's story of Peter's denial is also similar to Mark's, but Luke adds a personal touch by writing of Jesus looking at Peter who then broke down.

Trial before Pilate
Luke's account is similar to Mark's, but Luke notes the charges made by the Jews against Jesus. Luke emphasises that Pilate found Jesus to be innocent and harmless. Luke then writes of Pilate sending Jesus to Herod (Luke 23:6–12). Luke had written of Herod the fox wanting to kill Jesus (see Luke 13:31–45).

The death of Jesus
Luke seems to have additional information to that given by Mark. According to Luke, Jesus prophesies the violent destruction of Jerusalem (Luke 23:30–32). Luke also includes Jesus' words, '**Father forgive them; they do not know what they are doing**' (Luke 23:34), and his final words are '**...into your hands I commit my spirit**'.

These differences show that Luke's Gospel was written after the Romans destroyed Jerusalem and that Luke was concerned with the idea of forgiveness. Jesus' first words according to Luke were about doing His Father's work (Luke 2:50) and Jesus' last words are about his Father.

The Resurrection

Both Luke and Mark record the fact that women found that Jesus was alive, that the stone was rolled away and that the tomb was empty. Luke records that two men reminded the women of what Jesus had said about his death and resurrection. There is an inference that He has appeared to Simon, but it is vague.

> This is significant for Christians since women were not highly regarded by men at this time and Peter was being singled out for leadership of the disciples, despite his betrayal of Jesus.

- Luke records more post-resurrection appearances by Jesus than Mark.

- Mark writes that Jesus appeared to two disciples who were on the way to Emmaus but Luke tells the story in detail of how Jesus appeared to Cleopas and another disciple who did not recognise him.

- The disciples explained how they were depressed by Jesus' death since they had hoped he was the Messiah who would set Israel free.

- Jesus told them that they were foolish not to believe the message of the Scriptures, that the Messiah had to suffer and die before entering the glory of resurrection.

> The story showed that even after being with him for three years the disciples did not understand the sort of Messiah Jesus was.

- Cleopas and the other disciple recognised Jesus when he broke and blessed bread with them and remembered that their 'hearts burned within them' when he spoke. They returned to Jerusalem to tell the others they had seen Jesus.

- Jesus then appeared to his disciples, telling them not to be afraid and showing them his stricken hands and side.

- He ate fish with them to show he was not a ghost.

Luke was reminding the early Christians of their belief that Jesus was really alive.

Luke also records Jesus' teaching that the events of his death and resurrection were a fulfilment of the Scriptures, and that the disciples had a mission to preach repentance and forgiveness to the whole world, starting in Jerusalem.

Jesus' ascension into heaven took place outside Jerusalem and the disciples were filled with joy and went to the temple praising God. Luke's Gospel therefore finishes where it began, in the temple.

PROGRESS CHECK

1. Give five examples of demands of discipleship in Luke.
2. Give an example of Jesus' conflict over the Sabbath in Luke.
3. What is stewardship in Luke?
4. Why should the disciples carry a sword on their missionary work?
5. What does Jesus say on the cross as he dies?
6. Who does Jesus appear to on the road to Emmaus?
7. How did the two disciples recognise it was Jesus?

1. Homelessness, poverty, prayer, service, listening to the Word of God. 2. Picking corn on the Sabbath. 3. Taking care of the earth and one's possessions, understanding they are gifts for a lifetime only to be preserved. 4. Because they might have to face great difficulty. 5. 'Father into your hands I commend my spirit' and 'Father forgive them, they do not know what they are doing'. 6. To two disciples, Cleopas and another. 7. When he broke the bread.

2.8 Matthew's Gospel

LEARNING SUMMARY

After studying this section you should know and understand:

- the identity of Jesus as given in Matthew
- the key teachings of Jesus as given in Matthew
- the key deeds of Jesus as given in Matthew
- the account of Jesus' death, resurrection and ascension

Gospel events from Matthew

KEY POINT

NICCEA candidates should pay particular attention to Matthew's Gospel, which is the key Gospel for that examination.

Prologue (Matt. 1:1)

A table of the descent of Jesus Christ, Son of David, Son of Abraham.

The Infancy Narrative

- Matthew's infancy narrative is less detailed.
- He tells the reader that Mary found she had conceived by the Spirit and that Joseph wanted to have the marriage contract set aside immediately.
- An angel told Joseph the true situation and Joseph took Mary home until the child was born (Matt. 1:18–25).
- Matthew has the story of the Magi (three Wise Men) who see the star which they believe signifies the birth of the King of the Jews and visit the baby bringing gold (riches), frankincense (Kingship) and myrrh (special calling). They warn that Herod is a danger to the baby and Mary and Joseph flee to Egypt until Herod dies (Matt. 2:1–18).

Baptism

- When Jesus goes to John to be baptised, John suggests that it should be he who should come to Jesus. 'Do you come to me? I need rather be baptised by you.' (Matt. 3:15–16)
- Jesus replies: 'Let it be so for the present; we do well to conform in this way with all that God requires.' (Matt. 3:16)

Matthew's Gospel is very clear from the outset that Jesus has been sent by God.

- As Jesus comes up from the water the heavens open, the spirit descends like a dove to alight on him and a voice from heaven is heard saying, '**This is my Son, my beloved, on whom my favour rests**' (Matt. 3:17).

Temptations (Matt. 4:1–11)

The account here is the same as in Luke.

Worship in Matthew

Praying in secret (Matt. 6:5–8). Jesus teaches that hypocrites say their prayers standing up for all to see. You should pray in a secret place with the door closed so the Father who sees what is secret will reward you. He knows your needs and you should pray thus:

> Our Father in heaven, thy name be hallowed;
> thy kingdom come, on earth as in heaven.
> Give us today our daily bread.
> Forgive us the wrong we have done,
> as we have forgiven those who have wronged us.
> And do not bring us to the test,
> but save us from the evil one. (Matt. 6:9–13)

Answer to prayer (Matt. 7:7–11)

Jesus teaches that a person only has to ask to receive, to seek to find, to knock and the door will be opened.

Fasting (Matt. 6:6–18)

Jesus teaches his followers to fast but not to be gloomy, and to show no sign to others, keeping it as a secret for the Father.

Authority

- Peter's declaration (Matt. 16:13–17).
- The Transfiguration (Matt. 17:1–8).
- Jesus' authority (Matt. 22:23–27). Jesus is asked by the Sadducees what the relationship of those who have been married to each other on earth will be after death. The Sadducees were trying to trick Jesus. They believed that at death the soul dies with the body. Jesus replies that after death people are like angels. Then Jesus says: 'God said, "I am the God of Abraham, Isaac and Jacob, of the living not the dead."' People were astounded at his teaching. Jesus showed that God was constant to all generations in saying God was the God of all the Fathers of Faith.

Beliefs

- Jesus proclaims the Kingdom (Matt 6:25–34). Consider the lilies of the field. Jesus teaches of the great love the Father has for all His creation and He will look after all His children. The Grace of God, the tenants in the vineyard (Matt. 20:1–16).
- The Kingdom of God is like a mustard seed (Matt. 13:31–33), a treasure, pearl, a net (Matt. 13:47–50).

- How people will be judged (Matt. 25:31–46). Jesus cautions followers that God will judge people, bringing to Himself all those who gave food to the hungry, drink to the thirsty and clothes to the naked and who visited the sick and imprisoned, for '...whatever you do for the least of my brothers you do for me'.
- It is important for modern Christians that Jesus teaches that care for others (neighbours) is the first duty of the Christian.

Community

- Call to discipleship. As in Luke and Mark, the fishermen leave their nets and follow Jesus (Matt. 4:18–22).
- The Apostles are commissioned and charged with their tasks (as Luke and Mark) (Matt. 28:16–20).
- Christians are to be salt, light and leaven in a community (Matt. 5:13–16; 13:33).

Morality

- **The golden rule**: always treat others as you would like them to treat you (Matt. 7:12). On murder, reconciliation, retaliation, loving your enemies, reproving your brother, refer to Beatitudes (Matt. 5:3–12).
- Concern for the poor and oppressed (Matt. 6:19–21). Don't store up treasure on earth; store up treasure in heaven.
- You cannot be the servant of two masters; you cannot serve God and mammon (Matt. 6:24).

Justice

- The law and the prophets. Jesus says he did not come to abolish the law and the prophets but to complete it (Matt. 5:17–20).
- Do not judge others; remove the log from your own eye before worrying about the speck in another's (Matt. 7:1–5).
- Pay the right taxes to the right person – to Caesar what is Caesar's and to God what is God's (Matt. 22:15–22).

Lifestyle and social practices

Christian values:

- Do good secretly (Matt. 6:1–4).
- Honesty (Matt. 5:33–37).
- Beatitudes (Matt. 5:3–12).
- Taking up the cross – suffering (Matt. 16:21–26).
- Entering by the narrow gate (Matt. 7:13–14).
- Acting on the message. The man who acts on the words of Jesus is like a man who builds his house on a rock – his house has firm foundations (Matt. 7:24–29).

The Beatitudes (Matt. 5:3–12)

The Beatitudes stand with the two great commandments as essential teachings about what is important for followers of Jesus. They are teachings about the way Christians should live and can be applied to all areas of individual and corporate lifestyles.

> How blest are those who know their need of God; the Kingdom of God is theirs. How blest are the sorrowful; they shall find consolation.
>
> How blest are those of gentle spirit; they shall have the earth for their possession. How blest are those who hunger and thirst to see right prevail; they shall be satisfied. How blest are those who show mercy; mercy shall be shown them.
>
> How blest are those whose hearts are pure; they shall see God. How blest are the peacemakers; God shall call them His sons.
>
> How blest are those who have suffered persecution for the cause of right; the Kingdom of God is theirs.
>
> How blest you are when you suffer insults and persecution and every kind of calumny for my sake. Accept it with gladness and exultation, for you have a rich reward in heaven in the same way they persecuted the prophets before you. (Matt. 5:3–12)

The agony in the Garden of Gethsemane (Matt. 26:36–41)

- Jesus went to pray in Gethsemane. He told his disciples to wait for him and took Peter and the sons of Zebedee with him.

- 'My heart is ready to break with grief,' he said to them. 'Stay here and stay awake with me.'

- He went away from them and prayed to his father to take his cup of suffering away from him but ended by saying, 'Yet not as I will but as you will.' **He surrendered himself totally to the will of God.**

- He found the disciples asleep and chastised them saying they should pray they would be spared the test. He prayed the same prayer three times and each time his disciples slept.

> Matthew emphasises that the chief priests sought to suppress stories of the resurrection by bribing the soldiers. The disciples see Jesus and he sends them out to spread the Good News, to baptise in his name and observe all that he has taught.

Crucifixion

- Jesus foretells the destruction of the temple in Jerusalem (Matt. 24:1–14) and a time of persecution to come.

- He says there will be false prophets claiming to be the Messiah and there will be many battles, earthquakes and famines. His followers will be hated, persecuted and executed, **'and as lawlessness spreads, men's love for one another will grow cold. But the man who holds out to the end will be saved.'**

- The crucifixion account is as in Luke.

The Resurrection

- Daybreak on Sunday.

- Mary of Magdala (Mary Magdalene) and the other Mary came to look at the grave.

- A shining angel rolled the stone away; sound of an earthquake; the guards lay like they were dead.

- 'You have nothing to fear, Jesus has been raised again, come and see the place where he was laid.'

- 'Go and tell his disciples he has been raised from the dead and is going before you to Galilee; there you will see him.'

- They ran to tell the disciples and suddenly Jesus was there before them; he told them to go to Galilee.

- The guards went to tell the chief priests who bribed them to say the body had been stolen.

- The disciples went to the mountain and he told them, 'Full authority in heaven and on earth has been committed to me. Go forth therefore and make all nations my disciples; baptise men everywhere in the name of the Father, the Son and the Spirit and be assured I am with you to the end of time.'

Fig. 2.6 The Resurrection

PROGRESS CHECK

1. What do the gifts brought by the magi represent?
2. Which well-known prayer does Jesus teach the disciples?
3. What are Christians to be in the community?
4. What did Jesus say to his father in the garden of Gethsemane?
5. What does Jesus prophesy will happen in the future?
6. Who comes to the tomb?
7. What does the angel say to them?

1. Riches, Kingship and suffering. 2. The Lord's Prayer (The Our Father) 3. Salt, light and leaven. 4. 'Not my will but thine.' 5. Battles, earthquakes and famines, persecution and hatred; those who hold on to the end will be saved. 6. Mary and Mary of Magdala. 7. 'You have nothing to fear, Jesus has been raised again; come and see the place where he was laid. Go and tell the disciples he has risen from the dead and is going before you to Galilee and there you will see him.'

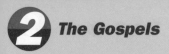

Exam practice questions

Short answer questions

1.   Total for this question: **19 marks**

(a)   Give the meaning of the word 'gospel'.   **(1)**

....

(b)   Name the two gospels that contain stories about the birth of Jesus.   **(2)**

....

....

(c)   What happened when Jesus was led into the wilderness (desert) after his baptism?   **(1)**

....

(d)   Which two people from the Old Testament 'appeared' with Jesus at the Transfiguration? **(2)**

....

....

(e)   When Jesus healed ten men of a skin disease (leprosy), only one of them came back to
      thank him. What was special about the one who came back?   **(1)**

....

(f)   Which meal in Holy Week is remembered in the Holy Communion service?   **(1)**

....

(g)   What are Christians talking about when they refer to the Ascension?   **(1)**

....

Exam practice questions

(h) Why were the Pharisees angry when Jesus healed a man who had a withered hand? **(1)**

....

(i) How might Christians show that they are not like the man in the parable
of the Rich Fool? **(1)**

....

(j) What does the parable of the Lost (Prodigal) Son teach about the relationship between
God and people? **(2)**

....

....

(k) At the end of Matthew's gospel, Jesus tells the disciples to 'Go ... to all peoples...'
Explain one way Christians have obeyed this command. **(2)**

....

....

(l) When Jesus was near Caesarea Philippi, he called Peter a 'rock'.
What might this event teach about the foundation of the Church? **(2)**

....

....

(m) At the end of Jesus' ministry, Judas betrayed him, Peter denied him and his disciples
deserted him. Do you think Jesus was a bad judge of character?
Briefly explain your answer, showing that you understand Christian teaching. **(2)**

....

....

AQA (SEG) Syllabus A, 2000

Personal issues

The following topics are included in this chapter:

- *The value of the individual*
- *Marriage, divorce and annulment*
- *The family*
- *Contraception, infertility and abortion*

3.1 The value of the individual

After studying this section you should know and understand:

- *religious teaching on the value of the human person*
- *the text of Genesis which describes the creation of man and woman*
- *Christian teaching on human sexuality*
- *Christian teaching on homosexuality*

All Christian teaching on human relationships is founded on the understanding of the nature of the individual person. Christianity teaches through the creation story in Genesis and through Church documents that each person was created as **unique** in '**imago dei**', the image of God. The fact that God was incarnated as human in the person of Jesus demonstrates the love of God for His creation.

> **Candidates must be aware of the need to learn specific quotes such as this and apply them to Christian lifestyle questions appropriately.**

'So God created man in his own image, in the image of God he created him, male and female he created them. God blessed them and said to them, "Be fruitful and increase, fill the earth..."' (Gen. 1: 27–28)

Human sexuality

AQA A   AQA C
EDEXCEL A   EDEXCEL B
OCR A   OCR B
WJEC
NICCEA

Christianity teaches that human sexuality is a gift from God.

'For this reason a man shall leave his father and mother and be made one with his wife; and the two shall become one flesh. It follows that there are no longer two individuals; they are one flesh.' (Mark 10: 5–8)

Sexual love

AQA A AQA C
EDEXCEL A EDEXCEL B
OCR A OCR B
WJEC
NICCEA

Sexual love is a powerful way of expressing love for another person. Christianity teaches that full expression of sexual love in sexual intercourse should take place in the publicly recognised permanent commitment of marriage. Sex before and outside marriage is considered wrong, as is casual sex or promiscuity (a series of many sexual partners).

A fundamental teaching of the Christian Church that relates to sexuality can be found in 1 Corinthians 3:16–17: '**You are God's temple where the spirit dwells.**' This, together with the understanding that human beings are unique and created in God's image, is the basis for the teaching which is that a Christian should regard the body as a sacred or holy place that should be treated always with respect. St Paul, in his writings, counsels against **fornication, lust, coarseness, greed and indecency**, and he encourages **fidelity, celibacy and chastity**.

> 'Surely you know that the unjust will never come into the Kingdom of God. Make no mistake: no fornicator or idolator, none who are guilty either of adultery or of homosexual perversion, no thieves or grabbers or drunkards or slanderers, will possess the Kingdom of God.'
> (1 Corinthians 6:9–11)

KEY POINT — An **idolator** is someone who worships idols or false, unreal gods, such as money, good looks or football.

Homosexuality

AQA A AQA C
EDEXCEL A EDEXCEL B
OCR A OCR B
WJEC
NICCEA

- Christianity recognises that some people are sexually attracted to the same sex rather than the opposite sex.
- The Churches do not condemn this but they do reaffirm the Church teaching of the **complementarity** of man and woman.
- The Roman Catholic Church teaches that **homosexuality is a 'condition'** which can be a trial and that persons of homosexual orientation should be treated with respect, compassion and sensitivity.
- The Church teaches that homosexuals are called to a life of chastity.
- In some countries, homosexual unions have been blessed by clergy of some religious traditions, but in Great Britain homosexual marriage is not recognised and therefore any sexual activity between homosexuals would go against Church teaching.

Homosexuality is a very contentious issue and candidates should be careful to be objective and measured. Refer to Church teaching, only give personal opinion when asked and always support your view with teaching.

● The Churches take examples from Scripture to support a condemnation of homosexual acts.

'In consequence, I say, God has given them up to shameful passions. Their women have exchanged natural intercourse for unnatural and their men, in turn, giving up natural relations with women, burn with lust for one another: males behave indecently with males, and are paid in their own persons the fitting wage of their perversion.'
(Rom. 1: 25–27)

PROGRESS CHECK

1. What is the meaning of unique in 'imago dei'?
2. What does Christianity teach about human sexuality?
3. What does St Paul say in 1 Corinthians about the body being a temple?
4. What wrong deeds does St Paul counsel against in 1 Corinthians?
5. What does the Roman Catholic Church teach about homosexuality?
6. What is a life of chastity?

1. The only one created in the image of God. 2. That it is a gift from God. 3. Your body is a temple in which the spirit dwells. 4. Fornication, lust, coarseness, greed, indecency, fidelity, celibacy and chastity. 5. That it is a condition that can be a trial and that homosexuals should be treated with compassion and sensitivity. 6. A life without sexual activity.

3.2 Marriage, divorce and annulment

LEARNING SUMMARY

After studying this section you should know and understand:

- Christian teaching on marriage from different Christian denominations
- the conduct of a Christian marriage ceremony
- Christian teaching on divorce from the Gospels of Mark and Matthew
- Church teachings on divorce
- the legal status of marriage and divorce in Britain today
- the human and social implications of divorce in society
- Christian teaching on marriage as given in the Gospels of Mark and Luke
- the status of annulment in the Roman Catholic tradition

Marriage

AQA A   AQA C
EDEXCEL A   EDEXCEL B
OCR A   OCR B
WJEC
NICCEA

KEY POINT

- Christianity teaches that the purpose of Christian marriage is for the mutual support of the spouses and for the procreation of children.

- Marriage is a legal status that is recognised by the laws of Britain. Every marriage must be officially recorded by a recognised registrar of marriages. This is to prevent the crime of bigamy (one person takes more than one spouse).

- A marriage in Great Britain is conducted between two consenting adults (from age 16 with parental consent) who are not already married, who are making the commitment freely without any pressure from family or parents and who are judged mentally competent to understand what they are doing.

'Every sexual act must be within the framework of marriage.' (Casti Conubii Papal Encyclical – Catholic Truth Society)

The Christian marriage ceremony

A marriage can take place as a separate service or as an integral part of an act of Christian worship. The latter is usual when both participants are Christian believers.

There are four parts to the actual uniting of the couple:

1. The minister establishes that the couple are free to marry and that no one has any lawful objections.
2. The couple exchange vows.
3. The couple exchange rings as a symbol of permanent love and faithfulness.
4. The minister blesses the union in God's name.

> **Marriage vows**
> I take you, [name]
> To be my wedded wife/husband
> To have and to hold
> From this day forward
> For better for worse
> For richer for poorer
> In sickness and in health
> To love and to cherish
> Till death us do part
> According to God's holy will
> And this is my solemn vow.

> Marriage is a very sensitive subject and candidates must be careful to separate personal experience of remarriage in their own families from the teaching that is set out by the Churches.

Christian teaching on marriage from the scriptures

Roman Catholic teaching is that marriage is a sacrament. This means it is taught as instituted by Jesus and therefore indissoluble (cannot be dissolved).

> 'Jesus said to them ... God made them male and female. For this reason a man shall leave his father and mother and be made one with his wife, and the two shall become one flesh. It follows that they are no longer two individuals: they are one flesh. What God has joined together, man must not separate.' (Mark 10:6–9)

Divadvance

Divorce

AQA A　AQA C
EDEXCEL A　EDEXCEL B
OCR A　OCR B
WJEC
NICCEA

Jesus went on to teach, 'Whosoever divorces his wife and marries another commits adultery against her; so too if she divorces her husband and marries another, she commits adultery.' (Mark 10:11–12; Luke 16:18)

> **KEY POINT**
> Divorce is the ending of marriage and, following the process, the previously married couple become single people again and are free to remarry legally.

> The monarch of the United Kingdom has to swear to 'defend the faith', which means the faith of the established Church of England. Prince Charles has already suggested that this should be changed to allow the monarch to be sworn as 'defender of faiths' as Britain is now a multi-cultural community with people of many belief traditions. However, for many believers this idea is too controversial.

- The Christian Church does not recognise divorce. A couple may be legally divorced but they are permanently married according to the Church and neither can remarry in church.

- The Roman Catholic Church enforces this rule stringently. The Church of England allows individual clergy discretion to decide if remarriage in church is appropriate. The free churches are also more flexible about remarriage in church following divorce.

- Prince Charles cannot marry Camilla Parker Bowles because, as a divorced woman, she is not free to marry and, as Charles will one day be Head of the Church of England, it would be difficult for him to be in breach of Church teaching. However, many people in their position are married every day in churches around Britain.

- The Christian Churches recognise that, while divorce is undesirable, the problem must be addressed. Christian Churches provide counselling and mediation for couples in trouble. They provide marriage encounter experiences and associations for divorced and separated Christians and single parents so that they feel part of the Christian community.

Christian teaching on divorce is given in the Gospel of St Mark. Controversy about the right to remarry is caused because in St Matthew's Gospel Jesus says:

> 'If a man divorces his wife for any cause other than unchastity and marries another, he commits adultery.' (Matt. 19:9)

This is why some Christians believe a marriage is dissolved if one partner is or has been sexually unfaithful.

> 'For married people I have a command which is not mine but the Lord's: a wife must not leave her husband; but if she does she must remain single or else be reconciled to her husband; and a husband must not divorce his wife.' (1 Cor. 7:10–11)

> 'You have heard it said, "You shall not commit adultery." But I say to you that every one who looks at a woman lustfully has already committed adultery with her in his heart. What God has joined together, let not man put asunder.' (Sermon on the Mount, Matt. (5:27–28)

KEY POINT — About 40 per cent of marriages in Great Britain end in divorce and this is having a serious effect on society.

- Children and adults suffer pain through separation and insecurity.
- The family home is often lost and two houses have to be kept, which is much more expensive.
- When parents separate and remarry they might have financial and care responsibilities for two families.
- Society often has to financially support victims of broken families.

Annulment

AQA A   AQA C
EDEXCEL A   EDEXCEL B
OCR A   OCR B
WJEC
NICCEA

Annulment is a means of having a Roman Catholic marriage officially recognised as void. It is not the same as divorce. It is a legal process in the Roman Catholic Church of recognising that no valid marriage has taken place. The most common reason for annulling marriage today is through proving that one of the couple was not capable of understanding the solemnity of the vows that were made or had no intention of ever keeping those vows.

KEY POINT Annulment means the marriage never existed; the couple were never married; the sacrament has not been conferred.

Fig. 3.1 A wedding ring is a sign of unbroken, permanent love and commitment

PROGRESS CHECK

1. What does Christianity teach about the creation of human life?
2. Where does St Paul say, 'You are God's temple where the spirit dwells?'
3. Against what does St Paul counsel in 1 Corinthians?
4. What sort of moral behaviour does St Paul encourage?
5. What is the purpose of Christian marriage?
6. What are the four sections of the Christian marriage ceremony?
7. What is divorce?
8. What is annulment?

1. Human life was created unique, by God in his image. 2. 1 Corinthians 3:17. 3. Fornication, lust, coarseness, greed and indecency. 4. Fidelity, chastity and celibacy. 5. Mutual support of the spouses and the procreation of children. 6. Freedom to marry, exchange of vows, exchange of rings, blessing. 7. Divorce is the legal severance of a married couple. 8. Annulment is the acknowledgement of a non-existent marriage.

3.3 The family

LEARNING SUMMARY

After studying this section you should know and understand:

- *Christian teaching on the family*
- *Christian teaching on the equality of the sexes*
- *Christian teaching on family and gender issues*

Christian teaching on the family

AQA A   AQA C
EDEXCEL A   EDEXCEL B
OCR A   OCR B
WJEC
NICCEA

Study the definitions given here and keep to the facts. It is appropriate to refer to personal experience but this is rarely credited unless it is used to support a point of view and referenced to a church or scripture teaching.

KEY POINT

- A nuclear family is the stereotype of mother, father and their own biological children.

- An extended family means a family that includes several generations of relatives, such as grandparents as well as uncles and aunts.

- A reconstituted family is a way to describe families where either or both members of a couple have been previously married and sometimes bring children of their own into a new relationship.

- A dysfunctional family is a family where relationships between members have broken down and none of the roles are clear.

Christianity teaches that the family is a good way of providing a stable and loving environment to raise children. The Ten Commandments teach children to honour their parents and the scriptures also teach parents: 'Fathers do not exasperate your children for fear they grow disheartened.' (Col. 3:21)

The Christian Churches also teach that the family should be the 'seed bed' of religious life. At Baptism, parents promise to raise a child according to the teachings of the Church. They should therefore teach the child to live by the Commandments, worship regularly and make God the centre of life. This is achieved by family prayer, attending church together, observing Christian social teaching by giving to charity and living a moral life, and taking opportunities to teach children the Word of God by example.

Practical support for families

- The Churches often provide practical help to families to help them to grow in their Christian life.
- The Churches support Church schools for the children of believers and also provide parent and toddler groups and children's liturgy, which help families attend services together.
- Many churches have traditionally been the basis of groups that support family life, such as the W.I. (Women's Institute), The Union of Catholic Mothers and the Catholic Women's League.
- Youth groups or clubs are often supported by churches to assist parents in helping their children to enjoy leisure in safe and suitable surroundings where they can meet other young Christians and form healthy relationships.

Roles of men and women

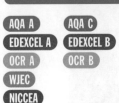

The Christian Churches have been accused of being sexist and **patriarchal**. This is because generally Churches have been run solely by men.

> Women should remain at home, sit still, keep house, bear and bring up children.' (Martin Luther 1483–1586)
>
> I permit no woman to teach or to have authority over men; she is to keep silent.' (1 Timothy 2:11–12)

Since the Anglican Church allowed the ordination of women to the priesthood, the Churches have been careful to point out the teaching about the equality of men and women.

> 'In creating male and female, God gives man and woman an equal personal dignity. Man is a person, man and woman equally so, since both were created in the image and likeness of the personal God.' (Catechism of the Catholic Church 2334)

St Paul taught that everyone is equal, Jew and Gentile, slave and free man, man and woman.

> 'There is neither male nor female for you are all one in Christ Jesus.' (Gal. 3:28)

- Christianity teaches that all people are created individually by God, in his image.
- It is appropriate for men or women to have any role in society that they feel comfortable with.
- The Roman Catholic Church does not allow women to be ordained priests because it says it goes against a 2000 year-old tradition and Jesus did not have any women as his disciples.

If you apply all these teachings today, you can understand that Church teaching has reflected the times. For centuries, people believed that women's responsibilities lay in the home and with child rearing. Women in the developed world are able to control their fertility and can choose to work outside the home. So, the Church has recognised they can have the same jobs as men. In the developing world, where fewer women are educated, many cannot control fertility and are less likely to work outside the home. If a woman works outside the home she can earn her own money, which means she does not depend on her male partner.

The Churches now emphasise the dignity of both men and women.

Fig. 3.2 A woman vicar

PROGRESS CHECK

1. Why is a family important in Christianity?
2. What do the scriptures teach children about parents?
3. What do the scriptures teach parents about children?
4. What does St Paul teach about the equality of men and women?
5. Why doesn't the RC Church allow women priests?

1. It provides a stable, secure environment for raising children. 2. Honour your father and mother is a Commandment. 3. 'Fathers do not exasperate your children for fear they grow disheartened.' 4. 'There is neither male nor female, for you are all one in Christ.' (Gal. 3:28) 5. There is no tradition of women priests and Jesus had no women disciples.

3.4 Contraception, infertility and abortion

LEARNING SUMMARY

After studying this section you should know and understand:

- *Christian teaching on the use of artificial and natural means of contraception*
- *Christian teaching on the problems of infertility*
- *arguments for and against abortion*

Contraception

 AQA A AQA C
EDEXCEL A EDEXCEL B
 OCR A OCR B
 WJEC
NICCEA

KEY POINT

> **Contraception** means against conception. It is a means of preventing a male sperm from fertilising a female ovum as a result of sexual intercourse, or preventing an already fertilised ovum (zygote) from implanting in the womb and becoming an embryo.

- Artificial contraception is practised though the use of the contraceptive pill, condoms, the inter-uterine coil, the diaphragm, the cap, the Femidom, contraceptive sponge and injections of contraceptive hormones. Their effectiveness depends on proper use.

- Natural means of contraception are based on knowing and understanding the female ovulation cycle. This can be monitored by chemical testing of the urine or through recognising physical signs of ovulation. Sexual intercourse is avoided at times of peak fertility.

Candidates might feel very strongly about some Church teaching on contraception but it is essential to understand the reason for those teachings and to present a balanced point of view giving both sides of the argument.

Church teaching on contraception

- The RC Church accepts the need to plan a family but states that every act of intercourse should be open to the possibility of children. The ideal is not to practise contraception but to use natural means as necessary.

- Roman Catholics must be sure that their reasons for deciding to use natural means of contraception are not selfish.

- Fertility is a gift and man and woman are co-operating in the love of God the creator when welcoming the gift of new life.

- The Roman Catholic Church sees artificial methods of contraception as intrinsically evil.

- The Church of England and other Christian denominations recognise the rights of believers to have children or not and to practise any means of contraception according to personal preference.

Infertility

AQA A   AQA C
EDEXCEL A   EDEXCEL B
OCR A   OCR B
WJEC
NICCEA

KEY POINT

> Infertility is a general term to explain that some couples experience a degree of difficulty conceiving children. It affects about 15 per cent of all couples at some time.

- Infertility causes great unhappiness to people who want children.
- The Roman Catholic Church is against treatment for infertility which dissociate the sexual act from the procreative act (test tube fertilisation) (Catechism of the Catholic Church 2377). It is vehemently opposed to embryo experimentation.
- The Church of England sees technology as affirming family life and providing opportunities for couples to be fruitful. It does not agree with payment for surrogacy. The Church of England supports embryo experimentation under strict control.

> 'Every human life from the moment of conception is sacred.'
> (Catechism of the Catholic Church 2319)

Infertility treatment is becoming increasingly high-tech and is removed from sexual intercourse (the procreative act as described by the RC Church). The most common methods include:

- AIH (Artificial Insemination Husband) – The husband's sperm is taken and injected it into the wife's ovum.
- AID (Artificial Insemination Donor) – A sperm is taken from a sperm bank when the husband cannot produce sperm.
- IVF (In Vitro Fertilisation) – The egg is fertilised in a test tube and the embryos are implanted in the mother's womb (no more than three). By law any extra embryos can be used for scientific experiments for up to fourteen days and must then be destroyed.
- Egg donation – A woman gives an egg to be fertilised and implanted for a woman who cannot produce eggs of her own.
- Embryo donation involves the implantation of a fertilised ovum from a donor egg and sperm.
- Surrogacy is the conceiving and bearing of a child for another person. It could be from the sperm of the infertile woman's husband or donor sperm.

> **Technology for artificial reproduction is developing all the time and candidates can achieve higher levels of response by drawing any recent cases into their arguments and applying Church teaching. The real prospect of 'cloning' human beings is a challenge to ethicists.**
>
> **An ethicist is someone who studies morality (right and wrong).**

Abortion

AQA A   AQA C
EDEXCEL A   EDEXCEL B
OCR A   OCR B
WJEC
NICCEA

KEY POINT

> **Abortion** is the premature expulsion of the foetus from the womb. This can be:
>
> - Spontaneous or natural – the foetus does not develop well or is damaged and dies and is then naturally expelled. This is called a miscarriage.
> - Procured through either drug therapy (the 'morning after pill') or surgical procedure.

Abortion is carried out in Great Britain in pregnancies up to 24 weeks if two doctors certify that the health of the mother, the baby or any existing children will be more harmed through the continuation of the pregnancy than through its termination.

Arguments for abortion	Arguments against abortion
Support for abortion is often termed 'pro-choice' because it is based on the ideas that:	Arguments against abortion are often called 'pro-life' as they are based on the view that life begins at conception.
• the foetus is part of the woman's body and does not exist independently of her • a woman has total right over her own body and has the right to choose to terminate an unwanted pregnancy • a foetus is not a human life, only potentially human life • women must have the right to safe and affordable termination of pregnancy • abortion must be available to women who are victims of rape • abortion has always existed and there is always a danger that women will be physically or mentally unable to continue with a pregnancy	• Human life begins at conception. (This is the teaching of the Roman Catholic Church). The occupant of the womb is always described as a child, not a foetus. • The potential child is genetically distinct from its mother. • Abortion is destroying hundreds of thousands of human beings who might go on to achieve great things for humanity • Abortion of the handicapped is an insult to all handicapped people who live fulfilled lives • If a child's life can be terminated at the point of birth, why not immediately after? • Abortion has a considerable effect on the woman often leaving her feeling guilty and distressed. • Abortion does not solve the problem of rape.

Abortion is a particularly emotive issue and many candidates will have very strong opinions and even experiences. It is valid to give personal experiences and opinions in the context of demonstrating knowledge and understanding of Church teaching

A child born at 24 weeks has a good chance of survival with special baby care. A mother can choose to have her pregnancy terminated up to the point of birth if tests show that the foetus is severely handicapped.

In Great Britain, there are approximately 190,000 abortions per year (1998) and the numbers have been steadily rising since abortion was legalised in 1967 (in 1968 there were 22,000). 89 per cent of abortions are carried out at less than twelve weeks of pregnancy.

Roman Catholic teaching	Anglican view
'Human life must be respected and protected absolutely from the moment of conception. From the first moment of existence a human being must be recognised as having the rights of a person – among which is the inviolable right of every innocent being to life.' (Catechism of the Catholic Church 2270) Abortion is always wrong even if the woman is raped or her life is endangered by the pregnancy.	'The Anglican view on abortion is that although the foetus is to be specially respected and protected, nonetheless the life of the foetus is not absolutely sacrosanct if it endangers the life of the mother.' (Church of England report, 1984) The Church of England teaches that abortion is always to be viewed as a serious matter. It takes a compassionate line and accepts that it may be necessary to avoid a greater evil. Abortion is acceptable if: ● the mother's life is in danger because of her physical or mental state ● the woman is a victim of rape ● the foetus is severely abnormal **In an imperfect world, a perfect solution is not always possible.**

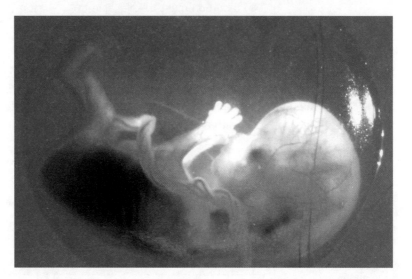

Fig. 3.3 A foetus in the womb at about ten weeks gestation

PROGRESS CHECK

1. What is contraception?
2. Why does the RC Church forbid artificial contraception?
3. What is abortion?
4. What is the anti-abortion lobby also known as?
5. What is the pro-abortion lobby also known as?
6. In what circumstances would the Church of England accept abortion?
7. Why is the RC Church opposed to abortion?

1. Contraception is taking action to prevent conception or fertilisation of an ovum. 2. All acts of sexual intercourse should be open to the possibility of new life. 3. Abortion is the premature expulsion of the foetus from the womb. 4. The anti-abortion lobby is the pro-life movement. 5. The pro-abortion lobby is pro-choice. 6. The Church of England recognises abortion as the lesser evil if a woman's life is in danger or she has been raped. 7. The RC Church is opposed to abortion because it teaches that life begins at conception.

Sample GCSE questions

Religion and human relationships

1.

(a) Give two religious teachings about marriage and explain what they mean. **(8)**

Christianity teaches that marriage is a permanent, lifelong commitment as expressed in the vows, 'to have and to hold, from this day forward, for better for worse, for richer for poorer, in sickness and in health, to love and to cherish, till death us do part, according to God's Holy will.' These vows reflect the teaching of Jesus, who said:
'God made them male and female. For this reason a man shall leave his mother and father and be made one with his wife, and the two shall become one flesh. It follows that they are no longer two individuals; they are one flesh. What God has joined together, man must not separate.'

All Christians believe that marriage is for the mutual support of the spouses and for the procreation of children.

(b) What does Christianity teach about marital breakdown? **(7)**

Christian Churches differ in their response to marital breakdown. The Roman Catholic Church and the Church of England do not recognise divorce. Roman Catholics can explore grounds for annulment if they believe the marriage to have been invalid. Anglicans who wish to remarry must seek out an individual vicar who is sympathetic to their case. All Christians are taught to view circumstances of marital breakdown with compassion and some Churches, such as the URC and other free Churches, recognise divorce as a regrettable end to some unions and endorse remarriage. The Quaker Church supports divorce as a means of avoiding further acrimony and bitterness when a marriage is spiritually ended or barren.

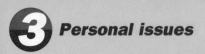

Sample GCSE questions

(c) 'Most religious teaching is against sex.'

How far do you agree with this statement? Give reasons to support your answer and show that you have thought about different points of view.

(5)

> AO3 questions are to test your ability to explain opposing religious arguments and differing points of view supported by knowledge and understanding

According to Christians, the first thing God said to his creation was to be fruitful, increase and fill the earth and He created humanity with the means to do this. Jesus points out that it is perfectly natural for a man and a woman to become one flesh. The Catechism of the Roman Catholic Church states that the conjugal act concerns the innermost being of the human person. Christians are encouraged to enjoy physical union.

The idea that religion is negative towards sex arises from the fact that Christianity teaches no sex before marriage and faithfulness to one permanent partner as well as opposing homosexual acts. St Paul instructs Christians to remain celibate if possible and talks about sexual desires as being lower than spiritual pursuits.

Religion is not wholly negative about sex but has guidelines for believers that help to protect people from pain, which can result from improper sexual relationships.

Chapter

Social issues

The following topics are covered in this chapter:

- **Old age, illness and death**
- **Euthanasia**
- **Prejudice and discrimination**

4.1 Old age, illness and death

LEARNING SUMMARY

After studying this section you should know and understand:

- **the mental, physical and social challenges of old age**
- **Christian teaching about death**
- **Christian responses to the challenges of old age, illness and death**

Old age

AQA A   AQA C
EDEXCEL A   EDEXCEL B
OCR A   OCR B
WJEC
NICCEA

KEY POINT

Old age is much more difficult to define than it used to be. Old age was previously used to describe people who had reached retirement age, which is currently 65. Many older people today live very active lives into their seventies and eighties, so old age often refers more to a person's capabilities than their chronological (age in years) age.

- Old age awaits every person.

'There is a season for everything, a time for every occupation under heaven. A time for giving birth, a time for dying.' (Ecc. 3:1–2)

- In old age, the physical process slows down, joints become stiffer, bones become more brittle, the skin loses its elasticity and people move more slowly and carefully about their daily lives.
- The rate of ageing depends on a person's genetic make up and on their lifestyle choices of diet and exercise.
- Intellectual capabilities can remain very good or can become impaired so some older people may be forgetful, confused or find everyday tasks very demanding.
- The longer you live, the fewer contemporaries (people the same age) survive as your companions.
- Very elderly people can be socially isolated as their partners, friends, siblings and relatives all die.

- The vulnerability of old age prevents many older people from leaving their homes so they lack social contact.
- Society does not always make good provision for elderly people so they are often left alone too much.

Christian teaching about death

- Christianity teaches that death is not the end of life.
- Every person has a soul or spirit that lives on after physical death.
- Christians live their lives in preparation for death, which is the time when they will become one with Christ Jesus and they do not, therefore, fear it.
- Christian belief about death is expressed in the Creed.
- Christians believe that all those who have died in faith have gone before them and are part of the 'communion of saints'.
- Christians do not fear death itself but individuals may fear pain of illness or an unprepared-for death.
- Christians like to receive the sacrament of the sick or the blessing of a religious minister when they know they are dying.

Christian responses to old age, illness and death

- Christians have their beliefs about death and eternal life to sustain them in their faith.
- The Bible gives very clear guidance to Christians about attitudes to old age, especially in the Ten Commandments – **'Honour your father and mother'** (Exodus 20:12).
- The Bible also teaches that you should honour your father in his old age.

Remember to use your own acquired knowledge in this area. Many local Christian churches have schemes to alleviate the suffering that might come with old age. Find out about them, read the local paper and be observant.

Practical responses

Christian churches often organise opportunities for older people to have social contact through:

- weekly lunch clubs
- excursions
- a network of visitors
- entertainment evenings
- social gatherings on important feast days, such as Christmas and Easter
- visits from the minister
- taking of Holy Communion by special ministers of the Eucharist
- arranging transport to church services within the community
- including elderly people as prayer companions for children taking the sacraments

• encouraging elderly people to be involved in the life of the church through different ministries

Christian Churches teach the importance of valuing every individual as a unique person created by God in his image and deserving of human and divine love.

Christian Churches also teach equality of all individuals in the eyes of God.

> 'My son, keep your father's commandment, and forsake not your mother's teaching. When you walk, they will lead you; when you lie down, they will watch over you; and when you wake, they will talk with you. A wise son hears his father's instruction, but a scoffer does not listen to rebuke. (Proverbs 20/21)

PROGRESS CHECK

1. What does Ecclesiasticus say about a time for everything?
2. Give two physical effects of ageing.
3. State two effects of ageing on the mental process.
4. Why might an old person be socially isolated?
5. What could a Christian community do to help an old person be more socially involved?
6. What is the basis for Christian teaching about old age?

1. There is a time to be born and a time to die. 2. Physical ageing causes stiffer joints, brittle bones, sagging skin. 3. Ageing can cause poor memory, confusion and inability to grasp new ideas. 4. Old people gradually lose peers, siblings and relatives, and are left alone. 5. Make sure there are opportunities to be involved in the social life of the community (see examples). 6. That every individual is created unique, in God's image and that all human life is sacred and every one is equal in the sight of God. Honour your father and mother.

4.2 Euthanasia

LEARNING SUMMARY

After studying this section you should know and understand:

● *Church teaching on euthanasia*
● *practical responses to euthanasia*
● *Christian attitudes to suffering*

What is euthanasia?

AQA A   AQA C
EDEXCEL A   EDEXCEL B
OCR A   OCR B
WJEC
NICCEA

KEY POINT 'Euthanasia' means an easy death.

> 'Whatever its motives and means, direct euthanasia consists in putting an end to the lives of handicapped, sick or dying persons. It is morally unacceptable. Thus, an act of omission which, of itself or by intention, causes death in order to eliminate suffering constitutes a murder greatly contrary to the dignity of the human person and to the respect due to the living God, his creator.' (Catechism of the Catholic Church 2277)

- Euthanasia is a word used to explain an easy death and it can be achieved by many different means.

- **Voluntary euthanasia** is at the request of the patient who asks to be helped to die, e.g. by asking for an overdose of drugs.

- **Involuntary euthanasia** happens when the sick person is too ill to make their wishes known. Examples of this would be:

  - Withdrawing an intravenous tube feeding a person judged to be brain dead or in PVS (persistent vegetative state). This is usually after discussion with close family.
  - Not taking efforts to keep the person alive by resuscitation.
  - Not treating complications such as pneumonia (passive non-voluntary euthanasia).
  - Giving drugs over a long period of time which control pain but eventually accumulate and kill the patient (active non-voluntary euthanasia).

> **KEY POINT** Euthanasia is a very controversial issue about which many people have strong feelings.

Church teaching on euthanasia

- The Roman Catholic Church is opposed to Euthanasia.

> 'Euthanasia is a grave violation of the law of God, since it is the deliberate and morally unacceptable killing of a human person.' (Papal Encyclical Evangelium Vitae 1995)

- Most Christian Churches are opposed to Euthanasia but some are more flexible about turning off life support machines or accepting suicide.

- Church teaching about euthanasia is based on the belief in the sanctity of human life as God's creation.

Examples

- Euthanasia is best explained through case studies because this exposes the human aspect of suffering and goes beyond the application of rules.

- **Tony Bland** was a football supporter crushed at Hillsborough who lived in PVS until his family sought permission from the courts for feeding to be withdrawn so that he could be allowed to die.

- **Annie Lindsell** suffered from a degenerative muscle wasting disease and applied to the courts to be allowed to die when she became incapable of moving. (She died before this became necessary.)

Candidates must look in the news for current cases that explore the area of euthanasia. New circumstances arise frequently.

Arguments for and against euthanasia

AQA A   AQA C
EDEXCEL A   EDEXCEL B
OCR A   OCR B
WJEC
NICCEA

Candidates must know both sides of the argument and use evidence to support a point of view and any recent case histories. Humanists also support hospices and believe in supporting life to its natural end.

For	Against
People should not have to suffer. Relatives should not see their loved ones in pain. Everyone has the right to decide when and how to die. Doctors should be able to judge the right time for a person to die. Euthanasia allows death with dignity. Suffering can be helped by drugs.	A sick person may not be able to make a rational decision. Doctors might take the easiest way. People are created in the image of God and life is a gift to be treasured. Energy should be concentrated on helping the dying.

A practical response

AQA A   AQA C
EDEXCEL A   EDEXCEL B
OCR A   OCR B
WJEC
NICCEA

- Christians are actively involved in the **Hospice Movement**, which was started by Dame Cicely Saunders.

- A hospice is a place that encourages people to actively enjoy all of their life.

- Hospices work with experts to control pain and to enable dignified death with the family closely involved.

> **KEY POINT**
> A living will is a written and witnessed statement that a person wishes to be helped to die when their illness reaches a certain point. Living wills are legal in the Netherlands.

Christian response to suffering

- The body is a temple of the spirit (1 Cor. 16–17) and life is sacred.

- How can a loving God permit the suffering of humanity?

- Humanity suffers because of the fall of Adam and Eve, which resulted in original sin.

- Suffering which is not made by humanity is a mystery.

- After death all mystery will be revealed.

- Christians must work through prayer and practical solutions to alleviate human suffering.

PROGRESS CHECK

1. What is euthanasia?
2. Name two main types of euthanasia.
3. Why might a Christian be opposed to euthanasia?
4. What alternative would a Christian offer to euthanasia?
5. Give the main argument in support of euthanasia.
6. What is a living will?

1. Easy death. 2. Voluntary and involuntary euthanasia. 3. Because humanity is created by God in his image and all life is sacred. 4. Hospice care, alleviation of pain, dignified death with family/community support. 5. People should have a right to end their own pain and suffering and to choose when and how to die with dignity. 6. A witnessed statement of intention for euthanasia.

4.3 Prejudice and discrimination

LEARNING SUMMARY

After studying this section you should know and understand:
- *the different types of prejudice and discrimination*
- *freedom of religious practice*
- *prejudice within religion*

> 'Every human being created in the image of God is a person for whom Christ died. Racism, which is the use of a person's racial origin to determine a person's value, is an assault on Christ's values and a reflection of his sacrifice.' (World Council of Churches)

Prejudice

AQA A   AQA C
EDEXCEL A   EDEXCEL B
OCR A   OCR B
WJEC
NICCEA

KEY POINT   Prejudice is shown by someone who prejudges a situation.

A man might believe he knows what another person is like because of what he has heard or been told about that person, rather than basing his opinion on what he discovers on meeting that person face to face.

Prejudices are formed in a variety of ways.

- Young children pick up prejudices from their home environment initially. Thus, if they hear others voicing opinions about particular groups of people they might form a prejudice.

- An adult might have had experiences of a person from a particular racial/ethnic or religious group and may then decide all people of that group have similar characteristics, which may be pleasant or unpleasant.

- When that adult continually voices that opinion in the presence of a child the child may form a prejudice. This is because the child has no experience of his or her own to form a balanced, informed opinion.

Examples

- A grandmother whose husband had returned, very ill and weak, from one of the Japanese forced labour camps operating during the height of the Second World War might continually speak, in the presence of children and grandchildren, of the wickedness of the Japanese. In this way a child might build up a prejudice against Japanese people in general.

- A family living in an area where a large number of immigrant families settle may find the different way of living and cooking difficult to understand and describe the newcomers as 'dirty and smelly'. Simply by absorbing this opinion a child could grow up with the prejudice that a particular group of people is dirty and smelly.

Negative prejudice

- We generally understand prejudice to be a negative thing since in an educated society it is regarded as desirable that children should be educated and able to make informed opinions.
- Chlidren should be discouraged from basing their opinions on prejudices they have picked up while young.
- Because it often stems from ignorance, prejudice is frequently accompanied or fed by fear and suspicion.
- It grows in an environment where exposure to anyone different heightens insecurity.
- Scapegoating is a feature of prejudice that is likely to happen when countries are at war or suffering serious economic decline, characterised by unemployment and poverty.

Types of prejudice

- There are many types of prejudice that are damaging to relationships in society.
- The very nature of prejudice makes it very difficult to re-educate people once they have an idea fixed in their minds.
- Prejudice is often reinforced through constant exposure to one-sided opinions at home.
- In the past, prejudices were often strengthened by careless portrayals of particular groups in films, on television and in books. Latterly, this practice has been carefully monitored by watchdog groups to try to ensure that every group is fairly represented.
- Unfortunately, some groups are not strong enough or do not have enough political influence to have their case put fairly and still suffer from prejudice in society.

 KEY POINT Typical examples of prejudices that people hold and which have been strengthened in the past by the media are gender prejudice and racial prejudice.

Gender prejudice

- Some people believe that women are over-concerned about home and family affairs and not about work and career.

> 'I permit no woman to teach or to have authority over men.'
> (1 Tim. 2:12)

- Women have achieved a great deal of equality in society and in the workplace but still do not have the same levels of pay as men.
- Gender prejudice is often reinforced by roles given to women in advertising.

Racial prejudice

'And if a stranger should live in your country, you must do him no wrong. The stranger who lives with you shall be as the home born among you, and you shall love him like yourself.' (Lev. 19:33–34)

Fig. 4.1 Racial stereotypes

'Black Afro-Caribbeans all listen to reggae music and smoke dope; they have noisy parties and are lazy and stupid.'

'All asians run shops, make money and live in large family groups.'

- This is the way these groups are often portrayed in the media and, although the music people listen to is an important part of their culture, and having a certain demeanour is also part of belonging, the stereotype does not give a true picture and reinforces negative perceptions.

- Surveys show that teachers often have low academic expectations of children of Afro-Caribbean origin. These expectations stem from deeply held prejudices. In theory, teachers should be educated and informed yet, even when people are informed enough to recognise and acknowledge their own prejudices, they are not always able to act objectively – subconscious prejudice may affect their judgement and actions.

- Asian people in Britain suffer more racial attacks than any other group.

- Portraying Asians in a particular way in the media has caused people to build up a stereotype and prejudge every Asian before knowing the truth. Many Asians do run shops but, like people in most other groups, they are also to be found in many other walks of life.

Fig. 4.2 A notice on a beach in South Africa during the apartheid era

Apartheid

Don't be afraid to use examples of prejudice from the media to illustrate your point of view. Always try to be aware of current events.

- One of the worst examples of racial prejudice was manifested in the apartheid system in South Africa.

- Each person was categorised by race: white, coloured or black. White children were brought up to see blacks as subhuman, unworthy of education, unworthy of a vote and not needing decent living conditions.

- Black people had to live in overcrowded townships with poor facilities. They were disenfranchised until 1994.

- The system meant that blacks had separate schools, transport, hospitals and eating places, and were not allowed to mix with whites.
- Relationships and marriage between races were forbidden and all blacks and coloureds had to carry a 'pass', which could be examined at any time; this showed where blacks were allowed to travel and work.
- Many campaigns were conducted in efforts to end apartheid and many people died in protests and riots.
- It will be many years before the prejudices, which built up among each group about the other, can be overcome even though the apartheid laws were abandoned in 1990.
- **Archbishop Desmond Tutu** campaigned tirelessly through speeches and marches for the ending of apartheid.
- **Nelson Mandela** (elected president in 1994) served 25 years in prison for his membership of the ANC (African National Congress), which campaigned for rights for black people in their own country.

Fig. 4.3 Nelson Mandela

Fig. 4.4 Archbishop Desmond Tutu

Class prejudice

- Britain remains a very class-conscious society.
- Every child is still labelled as belonging to a social group when he or she is registered at birth. The classification is based on the parents' jobs.
- The media portrays class in a very prejudiced way. The aristocracy is seen to behave in one way, the middle class in another and the working class in another.
- Thus we have prejudice about how people might behave depending on their status in life.
- During a time of economic depression, when the government seeks to cut spending on social services, we might find that certain groups are portrayed negatively in the media:
- A young, single mother might be shown to be living off state benefit in her own home and contributing nothing to society. Little thought will be given to the deserted wife or husband trying to keep the family together in the family home under great personal and financial strain.
- Similarly, old people might be described as living comfortably at state expense in a nursing home while the greedy family waits for him or her to die so that they can inherit the house.

Tony Blair (Labour Party) went to a public school. William Hague (Conservative Party) went to a state grammar school. This goes against normal political expectations. Candidates should follow trends in current affairs to keep answers relevant.

- The class system is still an important factor in the governance of Britain.
- A great deal of fuss was made about Margaret Thatcher being the daughter of a grocer and John Major being an 'ordinary' man, but still the majority of parliamentarians are from public schools and overwhelmingly middle class.
- Britain still has the upper chamber in Parliament, The House of Lords, membership of which is open mainly to the aristocracy, a favour usually conferred by birth, although sometimes by merit.
- This privilege of class is being eroded gradually as membership is replaced by life peers from all classes of society and walks of life.

Religious prejudice and the media

- Religious prejudice is reinforced through the media.
- The idea that all Roman Catholic families have dozens of children can be promoted by showing families with many children in Latin America without explaining the economic realities alongside religious teaching.
- It is also easily distorted by those who mock the Pope's teaching about contraception and by press reports that take lines from his encyclicals out of context and quote them without giving the whole picture.
- Jokes about Roman Catholicism and its stance on contraception can be heard every day. It is testimony to the security of the Church that they rarely cause offence. A presenter on daytime television, while watching a delicious 'diet' recipe full of bananas, rum and sugar, was heard to remark, 'This is like the Pope going for contraception.' An innocent off-the-cuff remark, which could be offensive, certainly reinforces prejudice but is unlikely to shake the Vatican.
- In popular culture in Britain – comedy and cartoons, for example – Jewish people are often portrayed as mean. Schoolchildren studying Shakespeare are exposed to the character of Shylock in *The Merchant of Venice*, who is seen as the epitome of meanness. He is so mean he insists upon a pound of flesh cut from near the heart to compensate for non-payment of debt.
- There is suspicion of religion in secular British culture. Religious people are often portrayed in the media as eccentric or out of touch with reality.
- It is also true that religious broadcasting is marginalised and reserved for late night or brief 'Sunday slots' on television. It is very difficult for presenters to give balanced views of the many different religious groups that are found in Britain today, and it is extremely difficult for non-believers to convey the faith of believers and probably impossible for non-believers to give a sense of faith to other non-believers. It is, after all, often difficult for believers to share faith together.
- Perceptions about religious believers are distorted by coverage of religious cults. These, and people who use religion for corrupt purposes, are given greater emphasis than legitimate faiths which have been practised quietly for hundreds of years.

Ageism

- Ageism is holding prejudices against the elderly – deciding that they cannot think or act rationally and are all physically frail, weak and not able to understand what is going on.

- It is also easy to see old people as marginalised simply because we are told they have no interest in the future, only in the past.

- Job advertisements indicate that, for some jobs, 25 or 35 is too old and those who seek jobs after the age of 40 or 50 can suffer terrible ageism.

- It is common practice to dispense with someone's services suddenly when he or she reaches the age of 65 or 70, and yet no one suddenly becomes senile because they are one day older.

> **KEY POINT**
>
> **Ageism is seen as a disgrace in our society especially by those of oriental culture who regard elderly people as wise and worthy of respect and honour.**

Disability

- We often have prejudices against disabled people.

- The disabled are under-represented in the workplace and the media, and disability is often seen as synonymous with stupidity.

- Because we have little contact with disabled people we act according to prejudice because we are not in a position to be informed.

Discrimination

AQA A AQA C
EDEXCEL A EDEXCEL B
OCR A OCR B
WJEC
NICCEA

> **KEY POINT**
>
> **Prejudice leads to discrimination – treating someone differently because of a judgement we have made about them.**

- Some potential employers might disregard women as serious job candidates because they are pregnant or because it is believed that they might have too many family responsibilities.

- In fact, many men and women have a very deeply rooted prejudice that mothers should stay at home to look after small children.

- This prejudice is often very subtly reinforced by advertising, which often shows the mother in the home environment or attending to children's social arrangements.

> **KEY POINT**
>
> **Discrimination can be completely unintentional, as people do not recognise their prejudices. It can also be totally, blatantly intentional, and insultingly so.**

- It is against the law to practise discrimination on the grounds of race, colour, religion or ability through advertising job vacancies, although in special circumstances the law can be circumvented to allow for special needs.

- Occasionally, for example, it might be necessary to recruit from an ethnic group for communication or language reasons.

- Many employers advertise themselves as equal opportunities employers and will sometimes mention groups that are under-represented in their workforce.

- **Actively seeking to appoint people because of their colour, race, age, gender or ability is called positive discrimination.** This is occurring increasingly as the number of people over 50 years of age increases; some employers are recruiting older workers, regarding them as more reliable and capable. Supermarkets, a traditional area for young recruitment, have increasingly looked to older workers to give stability to their workforce and to improve standards of customer care.

> **Look for any examples of changing employment practices announced locally or nationally.**

> **KEY POINT** Since October 2000, Membership of the European Convention on Human Rights means that any discrimination against people can be challenged in the European Courts.

Freedom of religious practice

- Religious freedom is enshrined in law in Britain through custom and practice.

- The US constitution states people's right to hold and practise religious beliefs but in Britain this freedom has developed and is cherished. Any religious group has the right to worship as they wish.

- Britain has large numbers of religious faiths. Each major town has many Christian churches and chapels, a Quaker Meeting House and a Salvation Army Citadel, as well as one or two synagogues (Orthodox and Reform), a mosque and a Hindu or Sikh temple.

- Each group holds its own festivals and believers are free to wear traditional clothes and observe feasts as they wish.

- Muslims keep Ramadan and other festivals.

- Jews observe Chanukah and all other festivals.

- Hindus and Sikhs observe Diwali.

- Children in schools with significant numbers from a variety of faiths are told about the various religious festivals in an effort to promote religious understanding and tolerance and to undermine prejudices.

Prejudice within the religions

- The Christian Churches have been widely criticised for what some consider to be sexual discrimination.

- In 1993 the general synod of the Church of England voted to allow women to be ordained to the priesthood after years of lobbying and pressure group action. Some members of the Church believed this was a great breakthrough for equality.

- Supporters of women in the priesthood argue that Jesus chose men for his disciples because he had no choice in the culture of the day and the Church subsequently developed in line with tradition so that women had a domestic or secondary role.

- In the 20th century women have the vote, the right to work, the ability to control their fertility and equal access to education and social freedom. They can be regarded as intellectually and physically empowered and socially more fitted to the ministry of the priesthood.

- Opponents of the ordination of women have argued that the synod exceeded its authority.

- Many members of the Church of England believe that Jesus instituted the priesthood through Peter and the Popes and only through the apostolic succession can women be admitted to the priesthood.

- The Roman Catholic Church remains opposed to the ordination of women. The Pope wishes to emphasise that men and women are equal but they have different ministries to offer. Pastorally in the Roman Catholic Church, many argue that women priests would not be readily accepted after a 2000-year tradition of male priests and the understanding that has been promoted that Jesus chose men.

- Fewer men are being ordained and many dioceses in Britain have a vocation crisis. Many Christians wonder who will be the ministers of the future.

> **KEY POINT**
>
> There are no distinctions between Jew and Gentile, slave and free, male and female, but all of you are one in Christ Jesus.' (Galatians 3:26–29)

PROGRESS CHECK

1. What is prejudice?
2. What is discrimination?
3. How do people become prejudiced?
4. How might gender prejudice be demonstrated?
5. Give an example of racial prejudice.
6. What is ageism?
7. What teaching might a believer use to reject prejudice?
8. What is positive discrimination?
9. In what way might the Roman Catholic Church be regarded as prejudiced against women?
10. Why do some Christians feel women should not be priests?

1. Prejudice is prejudging an issue. 2. Discrimination is to treat someone differently to another because of prejudice. 3. They form ideas about groups based on experience or reports of others. 4. Gender prejudice is not accepting that men and women are both equally capable of doing any job. 5. Racial prejudice is when a person is treated differently because of their race, e.g. in South Africa during apartheid. 6. Ageism is the assumption that people of a given age cannot undertake certain tasks efficiently. 7. Galatians 3:24–26 8. Acting against prejudice, choosing a person because of their colour, race, class, gender or religion. 9. By not allowing the ordination of women. 10. Because of the apostolic succession and 2000 years of tradition.

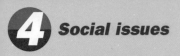

Exam practice questions

1. **Prejudice and discrimination**

   'I have a dream that my four little children will one day live in a nation where they will not be judged by the colour of their skin, but by the persons they are. I have a dream that one day…all God's children, black men, white men, Jews and Gentiles, Protestants and Catholics, will be able to join hands, and sing in the words of the black people's old song. Free at last, free at last, thank God Almighty, we are free at last.'
   Rev Dr Martin Luther King

   (a) Give an account of the Biblical teaching that Catholics might use in forming their views about racism and explain how these teachings are important for Catholics today. **(8)**

   ....
   ....
   ....
   ....
   ....
   ....

   (b) Describe how and explain why a Christian might help to fight prejudice. **(7)**

   ....
   ....
   ....
   ....
   ....

   (c) 'Women and men are not equal!'
   Do you agree? Give reasons to support your answer and show that you have thought about different points of view. You must refer to Christianity in your answer. **(5)**

   ....
   ....
   ....
   ....

Exam practice questions

2. **Life and death**

(a) What is the teaching of the Roman Catholic Church about life after death? (8)

....

....

....

....

....

....

....

....

(b) A Roman Catholic dying from a painful illness asks a close family member to assist in an easy death. What Roman Catholic teaching will be considered in dealing with this request? (7)

....

....

....

....

....

....

....

(c) 'The funeral rite is an occasion of great importance in Catholic families.'
Do you agree? Give reasons to support your view and show that you have
thought about different points of view. (4)

....

....

....

5 Justice and global issues

The following topics are covered in this chapter:

- **Peace and conflict**
- **Crime and punishment**
- **World poverty and environmental issues**
- **Work and leisure**

5.1 Peace and conflict

> **LEARNING SUMMARY**
>
> After studying this section you should understand in a Christian context:
>
> - the reasons for war
> - conflict resolution
> - the 'just war' theory
> - holy war, sacrifice and martyrdom
> - non-violent protest and pacifism
> - prisoners of conscience
> - nuclear war and disarmament
> - Christian teaching on forgiveness

Reasons for war and persecution

AQA A | AQA C
EDEXCEL A | EDEXCEL B
OCR A | OCR B
WJEC
NICCEA

> 'Where do all the fights and quarrels among you come from? They come from your desires for pleasure, which you are constantly fighting within you. You want things but you cannot have them, so you are ready to kill; you strongly desire things, but you cannot get them so you quarrel and fight.' (Jas. 4:1–2)

All animals compete against one another for food and territory. All creation struggles for survival ultimately to the point of conflict and death. The human animal is no different. Through the centuries mankind has developed methods of engaging in competition, which has grown more sophisticated, efficient and expensive.

Human beings go to war against one another for many reasons and increasingly the causes of wars can be seen to be a complex mixture of several factors. Some of the more obvious reasons for the outbreak of war between or within nations can be identified as:

- the desire for power on the part of an individual or a national government
- the desire for territorial gain
- the desire for (or need of) the natural resources of another country

- a build-up of armaments disturbing the balance of power
- a way of distracting the population from domestic difficulties
- the desire for national self-determination by ethnic groups
- a result of international alliances
- a result of military strategies or timetables

> **Take the opportunity to learn some facts about a current example of war in the world and find out the reasons for it by watching or listening to the news or reading newspapers.**

Examples of recent conflict include the former Yugoslavia where the individual races – Bosnian, Serbian, Croatian – each wanted their own nation state and fought to claim land for that state. In the war in Rwanda in 1994, the Hutu tribe attempted to wipe out the Tutsis in a bid for control of the country in which they both lived. The territorial disputes between Palestinians and Jews in Israel continue to erupt into violence and war.

Persecution

> **KEY POINT** Persecution is when a person or group deliberately singles out an individual or individuals and subjects them to planned cruelties.

- Persecution can range from name-calling through any manner of physical and mental punishment to genocide (the slaughter of entire races), as seen in the persecution and murder of the Jews in Nazi Germany.
- Often people are persecuted simply for being different; thus their persecutors are given a focus for their hatred. Or people may be persecuted simply because they are weak, vulnerable and without allies.
- Hitler had a charismatic personality and, by employing propaganda, he made use of natural prejudices against people who were regarded as different to scapegoat the Jews for Germany's defeat in the 1914–18 War and her economic problems in the 1920s and 1930s.
- Many Germans needed a scapegoat and Hitler was therefore able to embark on his terrible scheme to exterminate 6 000 000 Jews in concentration camps in Eastern Europe. **He called it his final solution.**

Resolution of conflict

AQA A   AQA C
EDEXCEL A   EDEXCEL B
OCR A   OCR B
WJEC
NICCEA

- Wars used to finish when one nation or party was seen to have won.
- This was achieved normally when the weaker side could no longer continue to fight because they did not have enough weapons or supplies for their armies.
- The winning side would normally make substantial territorial gains.
- In the 20th century some wars have ended (or conflict has been avoided altogether) because one side was able to threaten the use of vastly superior weapons, which would cause enormous suffering, e.g. the atomic bomb.

> 'How blessed are the peacemakers, God shall call them His sons.'
> (Matt. 5:9)

The United Nations

KEY POINT

After the Second World War, the United Nations (UN), was set up to maintain international peace and security, to develop friendly relations among nations and to promote co-operation in solving problems between nations.

- Most countries have become members of the UN. Decisions are made by the Security Council, which has 15 members.

- Five permanent members are USA, China, France, Great Britain and Russia.

- Any decision must be sanctioned by these members and any one of these five can veto a decision.

- Recently the world has seen the United Nations increasingly called upon to act to maintain peace and security. Increasingly, this has meant that serving members of the armed forces of member states have been sent to areas of conflict in the world to be part of a UN peacekeeping force or to help to secure the passage of humanitarian aid (food, medicine and shelter) to the civilians affected by conflict.

- The degree to which the UN is successful in this is difficult to assess. Some people feel it is not appropriate for the UN to be involved in civil conflicts.

- Sometimes the UN appears to have to withdraw without achieving its aims and sometimes it seems that the UN is drawn into a conflict on one side, thus appearing to judge which is the aggressor and which the aggrieved in a conflict which might have very complex causes.

- The most powerful member of the UN is the USA, which alone has the military resources to enforce any UN resolutions.

- A criticism of the UN is that it depends heavily on the agreement of the USA to carry out any of its resolutions.

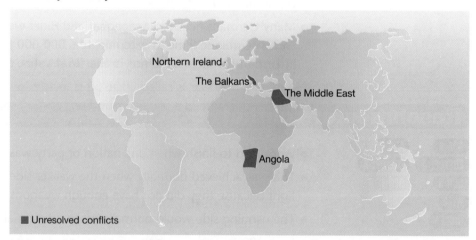

Fig. 5.1 Map showing areas of conflict in the world

Northern Ireland
The Balkans
The Middle East
Angola

■ Unresolved conflicts

Just war

AQA A   AQA C
EDEXCEL A   EDEXCEL B
OCR A   OCR B
WJEC
NICCEA

'It is lawful for Christian men, at the commandment of the magistrate, to wear weapons and serve in the wars.' (Article 37 of the Church of England)

- Christians recognise that war is not compatible with the teachings of Jesus, and theologians have looked for ways of reconciling involvement in war with their professed beliefs.
- In AD 400 St Augustine put forward ideas to support a 'just' war.
- This theory was developed by Thomas Aquinas in AD 1250. A Christian can look at these principles and use them to decide if a war is justifiable or not.

KEY POINT

The just war theory declares that:

- a war must be declared by a properly constituted authority, i.e. a constitutionally elected government, president or a sovereign in a monarchy
- a war must have a just cause, such as sef-defence or the reclaiming of lost territory
- a war must have a just aim and should stop when that aim is achieved
- a war must be waged justly, that is without endangering civilians (discrimination)
- a war must be waged without using undue force and without causing more damage than would have ensued from the original issue (proportionality)

Candidates should learn these clauses and think about how they are applied to any modern conflict that arises.

Holy war, self-sacrifice and martyrdom

AQA A AQA C
EDEXCEL A EDEXCEL B
OCR A OCR B
WJEC
NICCEA

'Declare a holy war. Call the troops to arms.' (Joel 3:9)

- Holy wars are so called because those fighting them believe they have God on their side.
- Christians waged 'holy' war against the Turks in the crusades of the 11th and 12th centuries to free the holy places of Palestine from the Muslims.
- In Islam a holy war is called 'jihad'; it is fought for the faith and anyone who fights is guaranteed a place in paradise.

Martyrdom

'There is no greater love than this, that a man should lay down his life for his friends.' (John 15:13)

'Anyone who wishes to be a follower of mine must leave self behind; he must take up his cross, and come with me.' (Mark 8:34)

- To be a martyr is to give your life for what you believe in, to die for your faith.
- This total subjugation of self-will is fundamental to Christianity and other faiths.

- The main period of Christian martyrdom in British history came after the Reformation. As Mary Tudor fought to reinstate Roman Catholicism as the established faith in England, many Protestants were put to death for their refusal to acknowledge the authority of Rome.

- Under the reign of Elizabeth I, Catholics suffered martyrdom because of their refusal to acknowledge the Queen as head of the Church in England.

- Jesus calls those who would follow Him to take up their cross and put self last.

- Every day many of the people who preach the Gospel of Jesus across the world put their lives at risk by presenting a challenge to governments. They call for justice for the poor in the name of Jesus.

- **Oscar Romero, the Archbishop of El Salvador, was assassinated as he continually spoke out against the government in the name of Jesus. He urged people to rise up against the injustice of poverty.**

Non-violent protest and pacifism

AQA A AQA C
EDEXCEL A EDEXCEL B
OCR A OCR B
WJEC
NICCEA

- Mahatma Gandhi demonstrated non-violent protest.

- He encouraged Indians to resist the rule of the British through passive resistance, by quietly ignoring instructions and laws and by not fighting back when attacked. He personally used to go on hunger strike to draw attention to a particular cause.

- Many Christians base their belief in non-violent protest on the teachings and actions of Jesus.

KEY POINT

A pacifist is someone who is against all war and physical violence under any circumstances. The Quakers are a group of Christians utterly opposed to war.

'Violence is the policy of barbarians; non-violence is the policy of men.' (Mahatma Gandhi)

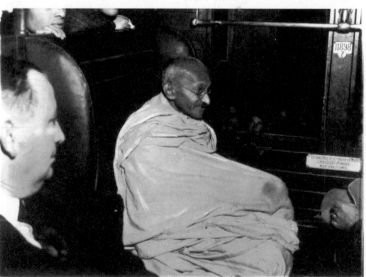

Fig. 5.2 Mahatma Gandhi

Gandhi advocated the same values as Christianity without being a Christian. During his life he was compared to Jesus. He lived poorly and had a great following. A person can demonstrate Christian teaching without being a Christian.

'You have learned that they were told "an eye for an eye and a tooth for a tooth". But what I tell you is this: do not set yourself against the man who wrongs you. If someone slaps you on the right cheek turn and offer him your left.' (Matt. 5:38–39)

Prisoners of conscience

- A prisoner of conscience is someone who goes to prison rather than fight for their beliefs.
- There are many such prisoners who have criticised their governments all over the world.
- During the two World Wars, men who refused to fight were sent to prison and known as **conchies** (conscientious objectors). In the First World War some were actually executed for their pacifist ideals.
- **Amnesty International campaigns on behalf of the falsely imprisoned all over the world and recruits people to write to prisoners.**

Human rights

'Each individual is truly a person with a nature that is endowed with intelligence and free will, and rights and duties ... these rights and duties are universal and inviolable.' (Encyclical letter, Pope John XXIII)

'No rights are possible without the basic guarantees for life including the right to adequate food, to guaranteed health care, to decent housing...' (World Council of Churches)

- The United Nations produced its Universal Declaration of Human Rights in December 1948.
- All the member nations agreed a basic code aimed at guaranteeing the quality of life for all their citizens.
- There are 25 clauses and the most important ones state that: all beings are born free and equal; everyone has the right to life, liberty and freedom from violence, and no one shall be subjected to arbitrary arrest, detention or exile.
- It is on the basis of the above-mentioned Declaration that groups campaign for freedom and rights of prisoners of conscience throughout the world.

You can find evidence of these campaigns in national daily newspapers in Britain and you should always look for current examples. For example, you could scan for newspaper headlines under which there is likely to be direct or indirect information on prisoners of conscience.

Violent protest

Terrorism is an example of violent protest.

- Terrorism is a form of war, which is not open warfare because the terrorists do not have a large and well-equipped army.
- Terrorists aim at any target, building or person that they believe will draw attention to their cause.

Look for current examples of terrorist activity around the world. Unfortunately, examples are always increasing and terrorists find new means of inflicting horror on the general public through hijack and hostage taking.

- Terrorism is seen all over the world. For people in Britain, the campaigns by Republican and Loyalist terrorists in Northern Ireland and on the mainland since 1969 are the most obvious example. Unfortunately, terrorists have now perpetrated so many atrocities that the unthinkable has become unexceptional. (The Omagh bomb in Northern Ireland in 1998 killed many children, babies and expectant mothers who were all innocently shopping.)

Nuclear war and the cost of war

'The monstrous power of nuclear weapons will have fatal consequences for life on earth. Justice, right and humanity therefore urgently demand that the arms race should cease ... nuclear weapons should be banned.' (*Pacem in Terris*, Roman Catholic Statement, 1965)

- All Christian denominations recognise that, even if a war can be called a just war, the cost of that war is a tragedy for the globe.
- The money spent on modern warfare would, if directed instead towards the poor, feed many hungry people and set up many life-giving schemes to improve the life chances of the disadvantaged in the developing world.
- Schools, hospitals, roads and factories could be built.
- The world has lived under the shadow of the threat from nuclear weapons since atomic bombs were dropped on **Nagasaki** and **Hiroshima** in 1945. That threat grows greater as more nations acquire nuclear weapons.
- All the Christian denominations condemn the use of nuclear weapons.
- In 1983 a Church of England working party report entitled *The Church and the Bomb* called for all nations to work together to reduce nuclear armaments; the report, however, recognised the difficulty of the unilateral option.

 KEY POINT Unilateral disarmament means that one individual country chooses to give up nuclear weapons. This was the policy supported by the Labour Party for many years, publicised by CND (Campaign for Nuclear Disarmament). Broadly speaking, the argument was that if no one began the process, disarmament could not happen.

 KEY POINT In multilateral disarmament the idea is that all sides give up their nuclear weapons at the same time. The thinking is that this method would not leave any countries vulnerable to attack by nuclear weapons while stockpiles were being diminished.

Fig. 5.3 Mushroom cloud over Hiroshima

Christian views on peace and forgiveness

- Christians campaign against war and violence in various ways and to varying degrees.
- Some Christians accept some wars as justifiable and some accept violent punishment as the only means of dealing with certain criminals. These Christians use different examples from Scripture to explain their position and different Church teachings.
- Christians can go to the Old Testament and find words to justify war as well as to support opposition to war.

'They shall beat their swords into plough shares and their spears into pruning knives; nation shall not lift sword against nation nor ever again be trained for war.' (Mic. 4:3–4)

'Is not this what I require of you as a fast: to loose the fetters of injustice, to untie the knots of the yoke, to snap every yoke and set free those who have been crushed?' (Is. 58:6–7).

'I remitted the whole of your debt when you appealed to me; were you not bound to show your fellow servant the same pity as I showed you?' (Matt. 18:32–34)

'Your brother here was dead and has come back to life, was lost and is found.' (Luke 15:32, The Prodigal Son)

'The generals are regarded as clever men. They commission powerful weapons and calculate how to kill thousands of people. Can there be any greater foolishness than this?' (Rabbi Nachman of Breslov, 1772–1810)

- Overwhelmingly in the Gospels, Jesus' message is one of peace and forgiveness.
- In the Great Commandments Jesus says, '**You must love your neighbour as yourself**' (Mark 12:31). The Parable of the Good Samaritan in Luke makes it clear that everyone is a neighbour.
- On the subject of physical violence, Jesus says, '**Put your sword back in its place. All who take the sword will die by the sword**' (Matt. 26:52). Jesus tells his followers to forgive. Peter came up and asked him, '**Lord, How often am I to forgive my brother if he goes on wronging me?**' Jesus replied, '**I do not say seven times; I say seventy times seven.**'

> **KEY POINT**
>
> All Christians believe that Jesus has secured absolute and ultimate peace for them by the supreme sacrifice of his death on the cross. Because the death of Christ assured salvation and his resurrection promised eternal life, Christians place their faith in the world to come. St Paul wrote, 'On the cross, Christ stripped the spiritual rulers and authorities of their power.'

PROGRESS CHECK

1. Name two major causes of conflict today.
2. Why might a person or group be persecuted?
3. What is nationalism?
4. What is pacifism?
5. Which Christian group is completely opposed to war?
6. What method did Gandhi promote?
7. What is the purpose of the United Nations?
8. What are the clauses of the 'just war' theory?
9. Why could a nuclear war never be just?
10. What is Christian teaching about forgiveness?

1. National self-determination; territorial gain. (There are others – see list.) 2. Because they are different, seen as outsiders. 3. Promotion of one nation. 4. Resistance to all violence. 5. Quakers (Society of Friends). 6. Non-violent, non-co-operation. 7. To mediate between nations and ensure protection of innocent victims of war. 8. Lawful authority, just cause, just intention, just method (discrimination), proportionality. 9. It cannot be discriminate or proportionate. 10. Turn the other cheek. (There are others – see above.)

5.2 Crime and punishment

LEARNING SUMMARY

After studying this section you should understand in a Christian context:

- **reasons for the existence of laws**
- **the difference between state law and religious law**
- **reasons why people commit crimes**
- **control of criminals**
- **forgiveness and reconciliation**

The existence of laws

AQA A   AQA C
EDEXCEL A   EDEXCEL B
OCR A   OCR B
WJEC
NICCEA

> 'Pay Caesar what is due to Caesar and pay God what is due to God.'
> (Mark 12:17)

- Laws have been established by human society to govern conduct.
- The type and nature of law depends on the type and nature of government.
- An elected government in a culturally Christian country might be expected to have different laws from those of a non-elective dictatorship in a totalitarian state.
- In Great Britain the elected Parliament proposes and passes laws and, in theory, these laws arise out of a fundamentally Christian culture.

- Many laws exist to establish 'a rule of law' under which all members of society are protected and are entitled to equal treatment.

>
> **KEY POINT**
>
> Laws are designed to protect the vulnerable so that human society is raised above a basic situation in which the 'law of the jungle' applies and the rule is 'survival of the fittest'.

Statute books are the books that record all laws made by Parliament.

- Thus, in Great Britain there exists a series of statutory laws which have been passed by Parliament and written into the **statute books.**
- These laws are enforced by the police and interpreted by the judiciary (the system of courts and judges).

Religious law and state law

AQA A   AQA C
EDEXCEL A   EDEXCEL B
OCR A   OCR B
WJEC
NICCEA

> '... you must obey the authorities – not just because of God's punishment, but also as a matter of conscience.' (Rom. 13:5)

- Although Britain is a state with an established Church, the Church of England, it is not true to say that religious law is state law.
- Many state laws are based on Christian principles but the two are separate.
- It is possible to sin without committing a crime.
- A crime is deemed to have been committed when someone transgresses the state law.
- Religious laws are a facet of each particular religion.
- Christian laws are commandments of Jesus.
- Christians are obliged to follow the rules Jesus has set out for them, particularly the Ten Commandments and the two great commandments.
- Each denomination has clarified certain transgressions that are regarded as sins. To sin is to ignore the laws of Jesus and in effect to turn away from him by one's own actions.

Young Christians today are not always familiar with ideas of wrong as 'sin'. Sin or wrong is turning away from Christ and this can be a deliberate rejection, as in the description of a 'mortal sin', which is used in the Roman Catholic tradition.

>
> **KEY POINT**
>
> In the Roman Catholic tradition, sin can be either 'venial' (less serious) or 'mortal', which is extremely serious and involves grave matter, full knowledge and full consent'.

> 'For sin pays its wage – death; but God's free gift is eternal life in union with Christ our Lord.' (Rom. 6:23)
>
> 'A person will reap exactly what he sows.' (Gal. 6:7)

Reasons why people commit crimes

 AQA A   AQA C
EDEXCEL A   EDEXCEL B
OCR A   OCR B
WJEC
NICCEA

- The reasons why people commit crimes are very complex.

- Some people believe that human nature is naturally selfish and greedy and people will always compete with one another; they will always want to have more and be more powerful than others.

- **Sigmund Freud** was of this view and held that people had to be schooled therefore to live together in an amicable way in society.

- Others, such as **Karl Marx**, believed strongly that people are formed by the circumstances in which they live. Thus, if one belongs to an environment in which some members are better off than others and material possessions are held up as the most worthwhile criteria on which to judge people, then inevitably many of the disadvantaged will take whatever steps they see as necessary to find a place in such a society.

- If the underprivileged have a lack of education and have grown up in an environment that is brutal and violent, then they have very few means other than criminal ones of trying to grasp a place in the sun for themselves.

- The balanced view is that crime is the result of a combination of factors, which probably includes the natural predisposition of a person to react against the negative aspects of his or her environment.

KEY POINT

Within the Christian tradition it is understood that people have original sin. They are naturally disposed to sin and transgress law and must be trained through Christianity to reject these feelings and try to do good to others.

Control of criminals

AQA A   AQA C
EDEXCEL A   EDEXCEL B
OCR A   OCR B
WJEC
NICCEA

- People live so closely together in society that those who do not conform to the laws present a problem, as they threaten the lifestyle of the rest of society and sometimes the physical well-being of others.

- The laws are enforced by the police and those who are suspected of breaking the law are tried by the courts and, if found guilty, can be punished by the courts. One of the purposes of punishment is to make a person understand the serious nature of his or her crime. The nature of the punishment depends on the seriousness of the crime.

'Then everyone will hear of it and be afraid and no one else will dare to act in such a way.' (Deut. 17:7,13).

Purposes and methods of punishment

There are different views about why and how people should be punished for breaking the laws of society.

Punishment can be:

- for **protection of society**
- for **deterrence** so others will be warned not to do the same
- for **rehabilitation** – to teach the criminal to behave
- for **vengeance** – to allow the victim or the victim's family to feel satisfaction that the criminal is suffering
- for **vindication** – to justify the existence of the laws

Common forms of punishment include:

- **a fine** – a sum of money is ordered to be paid to the courts, e.g. for motoring offences
- **Community Service** – the criminal is ordered to work in the community as punishment, e.g. for vandalism or anti-social behaviour
- **probation** – a criminal is ordered to report to a probation officer at regular intervals so that their rehabilitation within the community can be monitored
- **custodial sentence** – a criminal is sent to a prison or into youth custody

Corporal and capital punishment

Fig. 5.4 The electric chair is used for executions in some states of the USA

Capital punishment is the death penalty

- In Britain the death penalty was always by hanging; it was abolished in 1970.
- The death penalty is a subject of great debate and is seen as the ultimate retributive punishment. Opponents argue that in places where it exists (e.g. certain American states), there are more murders than in places where it doesn't exist.
- There are about 5000 people awaiting execution in various states across the USA.
- Gradually (as violent crime increases) more states opt for this punishment which is believed to be a **deterrent** and **retributive**.
- In the USA it costs more to execute someone than to keep them in prison because of the appeals process and lawyers' fees. Many people wait for years before the sentence is carried out. This is done by hanging, shooting, gassing, the electric chair or lethal injection.

Corporal punishment

- It is against the law in Britain for teachers to inflict corporal (i.e. physical) punishment on students and there is a strong lobby campaigning to stop all physical punishment.

- Recent judgements in the courts have mainly upheld the right of parents to use reasonable physical force when chastising their own children, but some parents have been prosecuted for hitting their own children, even though they maintained it was only for discipline and did not constitute abuse or cruelty.

Forgiveness and reconciliation

AQA A AQA C
EDEXCEL A EDEXCEL B
OCR A OCR B
WJEC
NICCEA

'If anyone slaps you on the right cheek let him slap you on the left cheek too.' (Matt. 5:38–39)

- Within Christianity there exists the belief that reconciliation between criminal and victim and society should always be sought and that punishment should be designed to rehabilitate the offender. Attempts should be made to understand the circumstances that led to his or her criminality and then efforts should be made to amend those circumstances, helping the offender to become a law-abiding member of society.

'Whoever sheds the blood of man by man shall his blood be shed.' (Gen. 9:6)

'And that is how my father will deal with you unless you each forgive your brother from your hearts.' (Matt. 18:35).

'I tell you this: whatever you forbid on earth shall be forbidden in heaven, and whatever you allow on earth shall be allowed in heaven.' (Matt. 18:18)

You must look out for specific examples in the news which demonstrate ideas about punishment. The case of Myra Hindley (the Moors Murderess) has been commented on for over 30 years. The case of the Jamie Bulger killers will also be debated for decades.

- Christianity teaches that wrongs should be forgiven.
- This does not preclude punishment.
- In the Roman and Anglo-Catholic tradition it is taught that reconciliation is a sacrament during which the repentant sinner:
  - acknowledges a wrong
  - expresses sorrow
  - accepts penance
  - and firmly resolves not to do wrong again

1. What are statutory laws?
2. What are sins?
3. How is it possible to sin without committing a crime?
4. What is the basis of law in England?
5. What is 'original sin'?
6. Why might someone feel obliged to break the law?
7. What are the purposes of punishment?
8. What sorts of punishment exist in the UK?
9. What is capital punishment?
10. What is corporal punishment?

1. Laws which are passed by Parliament and written in the statute books. 2. Wrong deeds that alienate a believer from God. 3. In the UK adultery is a sin but not a crime. 4. The Ten Commandments. 5. The first sin committed by Adam and Eve who ignored God's instruction not to touch the forbidden tree. 6. To register a protest against what they regarded as an unjust law. 7. Reform, deterrence, protection, retribution, vindication. 8. Fines, probation, community service, custodial sentence. 9. The death penalty. 10. Physical punishment, such as flogging.

5.3 Work and leisure

LEARNING SUMMARY

After studying this section you should understand in a Christian context:

● *what work is*
● *why work is important to Christians*
● *the significance of leisure time*
● *employment and unemployment*
● *acceptable professions for Christians*

'Our brothers, we command you in the name of Our Lord Jesus Christ to keep away from all brothers who are living a lazy life... We were not lazy when we were with you. We kept working day and night so as not to be an expense to any of you.' (2 Thes. 3:6–8)

'Work is a good thing for man – a good thing for his humanity – because through work man not only transforms nature, adapting it to his own needs, but he also achieves fulfilment as a human being and, indeed, in a sense becomes a "more human being".' (The teachings of John Paul II – Human Work, The Catholic Truth Society, 1982)

'I have come in order that you might have life – life in its fullness.' (John 10:10)

'Let us go off by ourselves to some place where we will be alone and you can rest for a while.' (Mark 6:31)

What is work?

AQA A   AQA C
EDEXCEL A   EDEXCEL B
OCR A   OCR B
WJEC
NICCEA

- Work is an essential part of life.

- For many people work is what they get paid for but work can also be unpaid, e.g. looking after children at home or voluntary work.

- A basic Christian traditional belief is that work is a means of taking part in the creative work of God.

- In the book of Genesis, Adam and Eve are given the Garden of Eden and told to till it and care for it.

- Pope John Paul II explains that work helps mankind transform nature, adapting it to his own needs, and that it helps people to achieve their potential.

- St Paul told the Christians of Ephesus that they should work hard and with gladness all the time, as though working for Christ.

- Sometimes, however, work can be tiring or painful. In the Marxist tradition, work is regarded as something that dehumanises the worker. It is not seen as a means to fulfilment but rather a means of control.

The right to work

- According to Christian teaching, every human being has the right to become a fulfilled person.

- The loss of a job often leads to poverty for the worker and the whole family is affected.

- Work brings people into relationships with others and lends a sense of community by giving people a place and status in society; work enables people to provide for their families.

- Christian teaching is opposed to discrimination on the grounds of race, age, gender, religion or colour in employment.

Leisure

- The importance of using leisure time properly is central to the Christian tradition.

> **KEY POINT** The Genesis creation story tells of God resting on the seventh day after his six-day work of creating the world. This is the origin of the Sabbath being a day of rest.

- Sensible use of leisure time enables a person to become re-created and more human, thus sharing in the creative work of God in the world.

- A Christian might use his or her leisure time to develop intellectually through reading or studying; physically through sport or dance; or spiritually through spending more time in prayer or service to others.

- Christians believe that leisure time can be used to help an individual develop as a person – to grow more human.

- Ultimately the Christian ideal that each individual grows more into Christ can be applied to each day. Christians are obliged to make everything they do a contribution to God's Kingdom.
- Thus Christians must recognise their gifts, give thanks for their abilities and use each day to work for the Lord even in a leisure activity. Through social clubs and contacts Christians can bring kindness to others and thus be witness to the love of God for His creation.

Vocation and career

- A vocation is a call. Christians believe that everyone is specially called by God for some work. Each person has a particular talent and should try to discern the particular work that God has set aside.
- This usually means finding paid employment in order to be financially secure and yet doing work that is suited to one's talents, beneficial to the family and community and in keeping with Christian ethics.

> 'A sense of vocation means we see what we do as an expression of our faith and a response to God's love for us. Ideally it should be possible to have a sense of vocation about the whole of life.' (What does Methodism Think, 1980)

- In modern society people are encouraged to have a 'career'. This means choosing an area in which to work and aiming to be a successful achiever in that area.
- Having a career does not necessarily mean not following a vocation. Indeed, many people follow careers to which they feel specially called.
- Having a career is distinguished from just working, which is seen as not fulfilling or satisfying. Yet some people with very simple jobs can feel called to their work because of the contribution they make to their own family and the community in general.

Acceptable and unacceptable professions

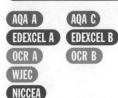

- For some Christians, certain areas of work are unacceptable because they feel those areas are not compatible with a Christian life.
- Many Christians would, for example, object to working in the arms trade or in a job associated with pornography. Christians might find working in family planning difficult, especially if it involved an abortion option. A Christian would feel challenged by any work that openly exploited others. Any work that is demeaning, degrading, evil or exploitative would be unacceptable to a Christian.
- Christians are often called to work in service, in teaching, medicine and social work. Most work is acceptable, especially if the primary purpose is good, i.e. service to others.
- Working in industry, commerce or banking services is acceptable as it benefits the community.

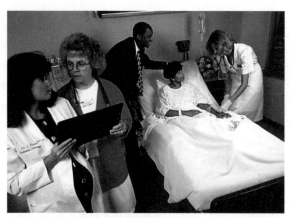

Fig. 5.5 The medical professions fulfil a Christian need to serve others

> **KEY POINT** Christians have a responsibility to remember that money, status and power must not become false gods.

Contemplative life

- Some people find that, for them, an appropriate way of life is to withdraw from society and spend life in silent prayer.

- There are religious orders that are contemplative. The Carmelite nuns enter convents and devote themselves to constant prayer as an interpretation of complete submission to the will of God. They usually work to support themselves by farming or producing goods for sale for the Christian communities. Their life is regulated by strict rule and a rigid routine of prayer.

Responsibilities of employers and employees

> 'Do not hold back the wages of someone you have hired, not even for one night... Each day before sunset pay him for that day's work; he needs the money and has counted on getting it. (Lev. 19:13; Deut. 24:15)

- Christianity is against cheating and profiteering through exploitation.

- Christians believe that employers have a duty to behave justly so they should pay fair wages and make sure their employees have healthy working conditions.

- According to Christian ethics, employers have a duty to protect the legal employment rights of their workers.

- All forms of discrimination are against Christian teaching.

- Christians believe that employees have an obligation to work hard, by using their time and talents to the full.

- St Paul told the Christians at Ephesus that they should remember they serve God through their work, not only their employer. The Bible contains many warnings against laziness.

- Christian teaching reminds both employers and employees that they should not make love of money and material things the prime motivation of work as this can lead to greed and exploitation.

Unemployment

- Unemployment is one of the major problems of modern times, caused mainly by technological and economic changes.
- In areas of high unemployment, poverty and crime often increase.
- People who become unemployed can often feel cut off from society.
- The psychological shock of losing a job can lead to physical illness.
- Christians regard unemployment as a social evil because of the loss of dignity suffered by the unemployed.
- It is sometimes possible for people who have become unemployed to regard this as an opportunity to retrain for a new job.
- Christians might also regard unemployment as an opportunity to reflect on whether God is calling them to new work.

PROGRESS CHECK

1. What scripture teaching might be used to justify the need to work?
2. How does work help a person become more human?
3. How can a Christian use leisure time beneficially?
4. What is a vocation?
5. What kind of work is unsuitable for Christians?
6. What responsibilities do Christian employers have to their employees?
7. Why is unemployment regarded as evil?

1. 2 Thessalonians 3:6–8 (see text). 2. A person finds out about him/herself and what s/he is capable of, thus becoming more human. 3. To serve others, to rest in order to work more efficiently. 4. A special calling through which a Christian serves God through serving others. 5. Work which exploits or hurts others or is against Christian teaching on human dignity. 6. To care for them, to treat them justly, honestly and fairly. 7. It takes away the means to feed and house oneself and places a person at the mercy of others, renders them powerless and robs them of their dignity.

5.4 World poverty and environmental issues

LEARNING SUMMARY

After studying this section you should understand in a Christian context:

- *the causes of poverty*
- *inequality in the world*
- *Christian responses to poverty*
- *stewardship of the earth*
- *environmental crises*

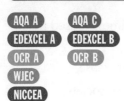
Causes of poverty

AQA A   AQA C
EDEXCEL A   EDEXCEL B
OCR A   OCR B
WJEC
NICCEA

- Poverty means to be poor and it is now recognised that people perceive their own poverty in relation to those around them. So poverty becomes **relative.**

- To be **absolutely** poor is to have no food, shelter or security. This is the situation for millions of people in the world.

- In Great Britain the government has established a certain standard of living which people expect. **Those who do not have the means to reach this standard are said to be living below the poverty line.** In Britain a poor person might have enough to eat, a home and even a car and many consumer durables; he or she could, on the other hand, be homeless and begging for money for food. In each case the person is poor relative to those around them, and according to life expectations and chances.

The developing world

- In the developing world many people have no shelter or food and little prospect of either.

- Many people do not have access to education or healthcare.

- They have a very short life expectancy (on average about 50 years maximum) and that life is often characterised by suffering through hunger and disease.

- Such conditions exist in much of the developing world, on the continents of Africa and Central and South America and parts of Asia. **This poverty is seen as absolute rather than relative.**

The Brandt Report

- **The Brandt Report** (1980) identified that the Northern Hemisphere, together with Australia, contained 25 per cent of the world's population and received 80 per cent of the world's income. This situation has not changed.

- In the north, people have access to education and healthcare and can expect to live for over 70 years. The countries of Western Europe and North America have most of the power in the world.

- The developing world has 75 per cent of the world population and 20 per cent of the income.

- People have little or no access to education, healthcare, business and commerce; they have no economic influence and can expect to live to 50.

Reasons for inequality

- The reasons for this divide are complex and any discussion of ways in which the parts of the world might be made more equal generates great controversy. Several causes of poverty in the developing world are generally acknowledged:

- expenditure on armaments (warplanes, guns and tanks/armoured vehicles) using money which is borrowed from the large banks of developed countries
- very large populations of very young children who cannot contribute to the economy

Candidates should look out for examples of factors that contribute to poverty or make it worse, such as Premier League football teams paying very low wages to workers who make footballs or shirts, which they then sell at inflated prices, making massive profits.

- world trade, which forces developing countries to sell their goods and services for very low prices
- high rates of interest on loans
- reduced level of aid from developed countries

● The developed world or 'First World' cannot ignore the developing or 'Third World'.

● The world is shrinking as a result of easier travel. Industries in the developed world depend on the Third World for raw materials and as a market for manufactured goods.

● Therefore developed countries are closely involved in Third World politics and economics.

● Many of the aid programmes are reciprocal so that money is lent in return for contracts being awarded to the lender country for other development projects.

● The countries of the developed world increasingly act as police (in the form of Nato forces) in disputes in the developing world. This might be to protect their own sources of valuable raw materials, such as oil.

Christian responses to world poverty

AQA A   AQA C
EDEXCEL A   EDEXCEL B
OCR A   OCR B
WJEC
NICCEA

'For when I was hungry you gave me food; when thirsty you gave me drink; when I was a stranger you took me into your home; when naked you clothed me; when I was ill, you came to my help... I tell you this: anything you did for one of my brothers here, however humble, you did for me.' (Matt. 25:35–38, 40)

● Christians are called to be closely involved with efforts to alleviate suffering in the world and to make efforts to work for a more equal world.

● The motivation for this is to be found in the Gospel teachings, particularly the commandment to love your neighbour.

● Jesus is unequivocal in describing people's duties to the poor. He tells the rich man to sell everything and give it to the poor (Mark 10:21). He condemns the rich man for ignoring the beggar at his door (Luke 16:19–31).

● In the parable of the Good Samaritan he demonstrates that it is important to have a care for all people (Luke 10:25–37).

● In 1 John 3:17–18, it is written 'If a rich person sees his brother in need, yet closes his heart against his brother, how can he claim that he loves God? My children, our love should not be just words and talk; it must be true love, which shows itself in action.'

'Go, sell everything you have and give to the poor and you will have riches in heaven.' (Mark 10:21)

- Christians recognise that they have a duty to bring Christ into the world through working among the disadvantaged.

- Jesus was always found with those on the margins of society: the lepers, tax collectors, sinners and the mentally ill.

- Jesus was insistent that the well did not need a doctor, only the sick (Mark 2:17). Christians are called to minister to the sick and poor.

Christian organisations alleviating poverty

- For the above-mentioned reasons, several Christian organisations were founded. These work to relieve poverty in the developing world.

- The Roman Catholic Church has **CAFOD** (Catholic Fund for Overseas Development), which collects money from churches, schools and other groups. Most of that money is used to fund development projects helping countries to build an infrastructure that will improve chances for the people.

- Similar work is undertaken by **Christian Aid**, which collects nationwide in May each year.

- Other agencies with a Christian foundation, which collect and assist in the developing world, are **Tear Fund** and **Trocaire** (in Ireland).

- It is also usual for individual Christian groups to raise money to fund projects or even send workers out to schemes and projects in the Third World.

> Candidates should thoroughly research at least one religious Christian organisation that works for the poor, either globally or locally.

- There is a growing tradition in which Christian Churches adopt a parish in the Third World just as towns are often 'twinned' with towns in another country. This is very effective if a member of the parish has worked abroad or the minister has personal contacts.

Christian teaching on poverty

> 'I tell you this, this poor widow has given more than any of the others; for those others who have given had more than enough but she with less than enough has given all she had to live on.' (Mark 12:43–44)

- Christians are also obligated to help others by Jesus' teaching about wealth.

- Jesus taught that people could not serve God and money. It is wrong to devote life to making money and acquiring possessions and wealth.

- In the Gospels, Jesus frequently demonstrates how he has come to be with the poor and how difficult it is for a rich man to enter heaven.

- The widow who gives more than she can afford to the poor is greatly blessed, more so than the rich man who gives plenty but has plenty to spare.

> **KEY POINT**
>
> Christian teaching on poverty and service to the poorest of the poor is increasingly becoming a 'gold standard' by which Christianity is judged. Jesus lived a radical life among the poor and many Christians feel this is the only way to be true to Christ's teaching.

Stewardship of the earth

AQA A   AQA C
EDEXCEL A   EDEXCEL B
OCR A   OCR B
WJEC
NICCEA

Fig. 5.6 Pollution from a coke works

> 'Be fruitful and increase, fill the earth and subdue it, rule over the fish in the sea, the birds of heaven and every living thing that moves upon the earth.' (Gen. 1:28)

- Christianity teaches that all that is on this earth is lent to the inhabitants for the brief duration of their lives.
- It is a Christian duty to care for the earth in the manner of a steward. Each person has a responsibility to help to cherish the earth so that it is preserved for the next generation.
- Many of the problems leading to the destruction of the earth can be seen to result from mismanagement of the earth and man's failure to act as a careful steward.
- In fact, man acts irresponsibly, destroying trees and materials that can never be replaced purely for monetary gain. This is unjust to those who suffer as a result of greed.

Dangers to the planet

AQA A   AQA C
EDEXCEL A   EDEXCEL B
OCR A   OCR B
WJEC
NICCEA

Candidates should be informed about environmental disasters, which occur regularly, and should listen to the speculation as to their cause, and use current examples in their answers on this theme.

It is possible to identify several major problems that are of universal concern regarding the destruction of the planet.

- The greenhouse effect causes gases to be trapped in the earth's atmosphere. This causes average temperatures to rise and sea levels rise as polar ice melts. Rising sea levels cause flooding. Warmer seas can lead to an increase in atmospheric pressure, causing hurricanes and typhoons.
- Environmentalists are also concerned about deforestation, which means there are fewer trees to absorb CO_2 (a greenhouse gas), and which also causes desertification as water not held by roots and topsoil is simply washed away so nothing can grow.
- The industrialised nations pollute the atmosphere with by-products of industry which contaminate the rivers, sea and land and cause the rain to become acid, which in turn poisons the land on which it falls.

- Humanity needs the planet and all nations to try to work together to agree strategies. Unfortunately, not many of the wealthy want to simplify their lifestyles and forego resources; so the poor need to take whatever chance they can to improve their standard of living. Thus, there is often a conflict of interest between governments and environmentalists, businessmen and the indigenous people.

- Governments are always seeking to strengthen their economies so they need to raise money.

- They encourage businessmen to speculate and invest and this sometimes leads to destruction of the environment rather than its preservation. In this way, governments and businessmen are often in conflict with those who live in the area. They wish to exploit original inhabitants.

KEY POINT

Christians believe there is enough for everyone provided it is managed properly. Those who have plenty need to understand that they do not have the right to more than a fair share. They must sacrifice some of what they believe to be a right, even though they have worked hard and see others having many practical benefits from a working life in the form of consumer durables. Christians should not live a life directed by profit motive and materialism.

PROGRESS CHECK

1. What is the difference between absolute and relative poverty?
2. How is absolute poverty characterised in a developing country?
3. How is poverty relative in Britain?
4. How does the developed world depend on the developing world?
5. How are workers in the developing world exploited?
6. What scripture teaches Christians to help the poor?
7. What is stewardship of the earth?
8. What are the major dangers that the planet faces?

1. Absolute poverty means no food, money, shelter or any possessions – utter destitution. Relative poverty means people have considerably less of these things than others around them. 2. People have nothing. 3. People might not have a car, video, TV or 'designer clothes'. 4. For natural resources, such as oil and minerals. 5. Through very low wages, no employment rights. 6. Love your neighbour. The widow's might. The rich young man. 7. Guardianship for your lifetime, care and passing it on to the next generation. 8. Deforestation, desertification, pollution, destruction of the ozone layer.

Sample GCSE questions

1. Peace and conflict

(a) Describe and explain biblical and church teaching about war and pacifism. **(8)**

This is a difficult question. It asks for recall of information and demonstration of understanding of how that information becomes Christian teaching and can be applied to real situations. AO1

- *Firstly, the Church teaches love of neighbour through the parable of the Good Samaritan, which demonstrates how even a traditional enemy of the Jews, a man from Samaria, helped his `neighbour´. Jesus teaches that everyone is our neighbour and we should live at peace with all peoples.*
- *In Matthew´s Gospel, Jesus chastises his disciple for attacking the soldiers with a sword. `Put up your sword. All who take up the sword, die by the sword.´*
- *In St Paul´s letter to the Romans he advocates that people should be kind to their enemies, not to seek revenge, and reminds them that the Lord says, `justice is mine´.*

Scriptural teaching is very clear about Christian duty to be peaceful and non-violent.

The Church has not condemned every armed conflict and has even supported the need to go to war to fight evil. The Roman Catholic Church developed the `just war´ theory, which gives criteria that need to be met if a war is to be seen as justified. The war must be declared by a legitimate authority, have a just aim and intention, be waged proportionately and with discrimination and have a good chance of success. The Church of England accepts that sometimes it is necessary to fight to defend a right or freedom.

Quakers are a Christian group that is totally opposed to war and teaches that violence is never justified, using the teaching of Jesus as justification.

(b) Explain how and why Catholics might support the rights of prisoners of conscience. **(7)**

This is an AO2 question, which means you must use facts to demonstrate your understanding.

- *Catholics would support prisoners of conscience by participating in the work of organisations such as Amnesty International, which provides lists of people in prison who can be written to. They also provide people who help with delivery of such letters. Through Catholic groups, it is also possible to visit prisoners of conscience. Catholics might campaign on their behalf by writing to the press or to governments.*
- *Catholics would justify this action by referring to Christian teaching, which advocates peace and could therefore justify becoming a prisoner of conscience. In Catholic faith history, there is also a tradition of martyrs who have died rather than compromise their beliefs and Catholics would use these lives as examples and inspiration.*

Sample GCSE questions

(c) Christians must use non-violent protest and never fight.
Do you agree? Give reasons to support your answer and show that
you have thought about different points of view. You must refer to
Christianity in your answer.

(5)

- *Jesus advocates peace and love of neighbour and the Bible urges that God should be judge.*
- *Christians have fought in wars for justice and the right to free people from dictators or oppressors and some Christians apply the `just war´ criteria to decide if fighting is justified.*
- *Quakers accept the strict pacifist line, which they believe comes directly from the teachings of Jesus.*

OCR Syllabus A Specimen Papers, 2000

This is an AO3 question. It seeks your opinion supported by facts and recognition of an opposing view. Use the information you have already referred to.

Say what you think. Was it necessary for Christians to resort to violence to resist Hitler? (Most Christians would say that there was no choice, although Quakers would say that violence is never justified.)

Chapter 6 Philosophical perspectives

The following topics are covered in this chapter:

- **The existence of God**
- **Religion and science**
- **Good and evil**
- **Truth and spirituality**

6.1 The existence of God

LEARNING SUMMARY

After studying this section you should know and understand:

- **the First Cause, the cosmological argument**
- **designer of the universe, the teleological argument**
- **the experiential argument**
- **evidence from Revelation**
- **atheism and agnosticism**
- **God and suffering**
- **God as Jesus**

Is there a God? This is the key question that has teased the minds of humanity for a long time. Religious believers believe there is a God and present many areas of evidence to support their belief, but they are always contradicted by those who say they can never produce God as evidence and therefore do not have irrefutable proof.

The First Cause

AQA A
OCR B

- Some Christians put their trust in the arguments of St Thomas Aquinas, a 13th century philosopher, who said that he could prove the existence of God.

- His main argument was that **GOD IS THE FIRST UNCAUSED CAUSE.**

- Aquinas pointed to the fact that the Universe exists as evidence, and people should ask how it came to be.

- Non-believers would counter that it came into existence as a result of a massive explosion called the big bang.

- Aquinas would have argued that something had to exist to cause that which led to the big bang and that first uncaused cause must be God.

> If something is ambiguous, its meaning is not clear or can be interpreted in more than one way.

- Thomas Aquinas seems to have put forward a logical argument but he does not convince everyone and doubters hold that his argument is not proof but is **ambiguous.**

- Some would point to a view that the advent of the universe is simply an unfolding mystery and no one has yet reached back to its origins. **It is a chain reaction, which has no starting point.**

137

Fig. 6.1 The origins of the universe, the big bang

> **KEY POINT** The First Cause argument is called the cosmological argument because it is founded in the cosmos.

Designer of the universe

'Ever since God created the world, his everlasting power and deity – however invisible – have been there for the mind to see in the things he has made.' (Rom. 1:20)

- Many believers would point to the evidence of the seeming wonder of the natural world as the proof that God exists.
- This argument was developed by **William Paley** in the 18th century.
- He used the example of a watch. If a man found a brilliant watch he would wonder who designed it, he would not assume it had simply evolved.

Fig. 6.2 William Paley understood the argument from design by looking at a watch

- Similarly, if we look at the animals, birds and plant life and see how each is brilliantly designed to fit its purpose, we must conclude that those things have been designed by a brilliant maker. Paley calls that maker God.

- Those who disagree with Paley would say that the universe was not planned but that it and all its creatures have evolved.

- Those that are not well adapted simply do not survive. As a result, what is left is the best example available. Classically the dinosaurs died out because they were not able to or 'designed' to adapt to a changing world.

- Similarly, many other creatures are now under threat because they are not well designed for the environment they find themselves in. The law of the jungle is 'survival of the fittest' and nature is seemingly very cruel, with some animals obviously less well designed than others.

- This would seem to point to the fact that the order in the universe is as a result of random chance, not clever design.

How convincing is the argument from design?

- In fact, if God did design the weaknesses in some of creation then He could be seen to have built suffering into the world and visited it upon some more than others. So Paley has proved nothing.

> **KEY POINT** The argument from design is sometimes called the teleological argument, from the Greek word 'telos' meaning 'order'.

The experience of God

AQA B
OCR B

- Many religious believers accept that 'God' cannot be produced but still believe in him.

- Some religious belief is based firmly on the individual's own experience of God which they hold to be real. **This experience can take a variety of forms.**

- **Meeting the 'numinous'** is when a person is filled with awe and wonder and an overwhelming sense that there is something beyond the self, something that transcends the human person and is infinitely greater.

- An example of this could be inspired by the sight of a magnificent cathedral, such as Salisbury Cathedral, bathed in the early evening sunlight, its spire reaching into the sky and absolutely dominating the beauty of the surrounding countryside. The cathedral would provide a living testimony to the belief of those, hundreds of years before, who wanted to provide a monument to God and did so in a way which has inspired generations.

Fig. 6.3 Salisbury Cathedral

A conversion experience is when a person is moved to change his or her life based on a sense that he or she is called by God to put faith at the centre of their life.

- This situation is often described by groups of Christians who call themselves 'born again' or Evangelical Christians.

- They have made a full adult commitment in response to a call to put Jesus at the centre of their lives.

- They believe they have personally been called by Jesus. This is also to be found within the Anglican and Roman Catholic traditions where people would not be re-baptised but would describe themselves as part of a 'charismatic' movement within the Church.

Witnessing a miracle is another way that people describe personal experiences of God, and there are plenty of documented cases.

 KEY POINT A miracle is said to occur when events happen which cannot be explained by any rational means.

- Occasionally people are cured from illness when conventional medicine could see no hope, and some people would explain this as a miracle. Miracles are mentioned in all the major faith traditions.

- Religious believers make pilgrimages to holy places where they believe miracles have occurred. Lourdes in South-West France is famous for miracles. The Virgin Mary is believed to have appeared there to a young peasant girl in the 19th century.

Experiencing the power of prayer can sometimes be seen as a link to a miracle.

- People pray for a cure and their prayer is answered. They see this as a miracle.

- Yet people can experience the power of prayer and witness no miracle. Some believers will describe themselves as being filled with a deep peace as a result of prayer.

- Some will declare themselves strengthened and fortified by their experience and able to face life more easily.

- A mystical experience can sometimes be part of prayer.

Candidates should look for examples from the media of people who have described a mystical experience or a vision.

- In some traditions, people pray by use of imaging, e.g. picturing themselves at the foot of the cross of Jesus. Sometimes believers feel they are in contact with God in a real and personal way.
- Believers sometimes feel that they have experienced God in a mystical way in seeing different visions or receiving messages.

The revelation of God

AQA A
OCR B

 KEY POINT Revelation means 'revealed' or 'shown' and Christians believe that God has revealed himself to the world in the person of Jesus.

- The love of God is shown in the teachings of Jesus, who came as God's Son to teach people to love one another absolutely and who showed his own love for humanity by suffering humiliation and death, taking all the sins of creation upon himself and ensuring salvation for all people.
- The love of God is also shown in those who live their lives in his name, such as St Francis of Assisi who rejected the world to live a life of poverty dedicated to simplicity, prayer and care for the poor and outcasts of society.

Revelation through Scripture

- The Bible is the Holy Book of Christianity and the nature of God is revealed to believers through the writings in the Old and New Testaments. In the book of Isaiah, God is revealed as ruler and judge of all.

> 'See how I lay in Zion, a stone witness, a precious cornerstone, a foundation stone: the believer shall not stumble. And I will make justice the measure, integrity the plumb-line.' (Is. 28:16–17)

- Through the many writings of St Paul, God is revealed to Christians as Saviour and friend.
- Paul takes the writings of the Gospels and delivers the Good News (that Jesus is Saviour) to many Christians. St Paul makes it clear that Jesus is the Son of God and has always existed.

> 'He has let us know the mystery of his purpose, the hidden plan he so kindly made in Christ from the beginning.' (Eph. 1:9)

The Gospel writers also made clear their views of God.

> 'Today in the town of David a Saviour has been born to you and He is Christ the Lord.' (Luke 2:11)
>
> 'When the advocate comes, whom I shall send to you from the Father, the Spirit of truth who issues from the Father, he wilt be my witness.' (John 15:26)

God revealed through religious upbringing

- Children brought up in a family of religious believers will be exposed to religious teachings about how and where God can be met.

- Strong adherents to religious faiths believe that it is essential to teach children about faith from the beginning and to welcome children into the religious community.

- In Christianity, new members are welcomed through an initiation ceremony of Christening or Baptism. Often this is in infancy when the child is claimed as one of Christ's family and promises are made on his or her behalf.

- The child is then raised in the way of the faith and all the Church's teachings are made clear.

- As the child grows he or she lives the annual pattern of festivals with family and friends, joins in the rites of passage, such as confirmation and marriage, and sees others in his or her family and community also following the same path. Many Christians take part in weekly services of worship and associate socially in church-based activities.

- When the whole of a child's community is involved with the same values and teachings, this makes for a strong sense of belonging and Christians put Jesus at the centre of that belonging in trying to uphold the values Jesus taught in the Gospels.

 KEY POINT — **Christianity teaches that Jesus is the way to the Father, and thus living the Christian life in family and community leads believers to God.**

Atheism and agnosticism

 AQA A
OCR B

- Just as living in a believing community may lead people to God, so living with disbelief can also influence people to reject the idea of God.

 KEY POINT — **An atheist is one who believes that there is no God. An agnostic is one who is not convinced of the existence or the non-existence of God.**

- If a child is brought up in an environment without worship or exposure to the experience of belief in God, he or she may find atheism or agnosticism a more realistic path through life.

- An atheist may be a **humanist.**

 KEY POINT — **A humanist is a person who believes that life on earth is the only life and people should live good lives of consideration to others to make life enjoyable and rewarding for everyone.**

Evil and suffering

Question: If God loves His creation, if He is all-powerful (omnipotent) and also benevolent, how can He allow terrible human suffering?

- Even people who have been exposed to a great deal of religious belief and practice, which may be very positive, can come to reject the existence of God because they fail to find or see Him. He is not revealed to them.

- One of the primary causes given for rejection of the idea of God is the evidence of human suffering, which can seem so contradictory to all the teachings of the Church about God.

- Suffering is often linked to evil, and the question of evil also challenges the minds of believers and non-believers.

- The existence of evil is explained in Christianity by the story of Adam and Eve, who fell pray to temptation and disobeyed God, and thus were rejected from God's presence. **This is called the 'Fall'.**

- **Christians believe that God created humans with free will** and they choose to surrender to temptation, which is the inclination to follow a path of disobedience to the will of God.

- Throughout Christian history, evil has been acknowledged as existing. Sometimes it is personified as 'Satan' and sometimes it is deemed the person's own weakness. **For many non-believers, the tangible evil that can be seen in the world is proof that God does not exist as a force of good anywhere.**

- Every individual must work out his own way of coping with the pain of his own suffering and the pain of witnessing the suffering of loved ones and of all humanity.

Christians have several ways of coping with suffering.

- C.S. Lewis, a well-known author (especially to readers of the *Narnia* books), was also famous for his writings about Christian responses to questions of meaning. He suffered the terrible pain of watching the woman he loved die in pain. He naturally thought about this terrible event and he wrote:

'Is it rational to believe in a bad God? Anyway, in a God so bad as all that? The Cosmic Sadist, the spiteful imbecile?' (*A Grief Observed*)

- Christians pray for those who suffer that they will have the strength to bear with it and also to ask (as Jesus did in Gethsemane) that, if it is possible, God will relieve them of the suffering or that they will have the faith to trust in God.

- Christians feel called to help those who suffer. A Christian life is one of 'vocation', a calling to do God's work. Christians try to work with those who suffer in order to help them.

- Many Christians also believe that helping others can often create a more humble and accepting attitude to one's own life, with all its positive and negative aspects.

For many Christians there is no answer to suffering. To see a child in pain or a mother grieving the loss of a child is to enter into the realms of a deeply painful mystery. Perhaps it is one people can only see when they reach the end of the Christian journey and become one with Christ and enter into his suffering as he entered into theirs by suffering and dying on the cross. It is true that, despite the terrible suffering people see and endure, many still find comfort and strength in turning to God. See, for example, the account of the crucifixion (Matt. 27:32–56).

> 'Yes, God loved the world so much that he gave his only Son, so that everyone who believes in him may not be lost but may have eternal life. For God sent his Son into the world not to condemn the world, but so that through him the world might be saved. No one who believes in him will be condemned; but whoever refuses to believe is condemned already, because he has refused to believe in the name of God's only Son. (John 3:16–18)

> 'They were still helpless when at this appointed moment, Christ died for sinful men. It is not easy to die, even for a good man – though of course for someone really worthy, a man might be prepared to die – but what proves that God loves us is that Christ died for us while we were still sinners.' (Rom. 5:6–8)

 KEY POINT The whole of Christianity is based on the sacrifice that Jesus made in suffering and dying to save all humanity and thus the Christian response to suffering is often to offer it up to God in love and trust.

The nature of God

 AQA A
OCR B

- Christians occupy themselves with imagery to bring alive the idea of God for themselves.
- Jesus is the incarnation and therefore the 'human' face of God.
- In him, Christians see God's qualities. This is the human dimension.
- But God is also **omnipotent, omniscient and Father of all creation.**
- Christians describe God as a Trinity: Father, Son and Spirit.
- This enables believers to have a relationship with God.
- The transcendent God is the Great God, the Creator God and the loving Father.
- Jesus is the way to Him. Jesus is the brother, the friend, the teacher, the man who suffers with all his creation. He is the immanent God, the God within.
- The spirit is the power of God through which miracles occur and which gives believers strength and courage to follow the way to Jesus the Father.

- The words that believers use to describe God help to make the doctrine of the Trinity more meaningful and more real.

- The writers of the various books of the Bible use metaphor, describing God as Father, Creator, and describing Jesus as Shepherd (carer for his flock), Teacher, Master, Son of God, Son of Man. The Spirit is seen as a dove, a flame and a wind and is therefore identified as being an unseen power or a bird that soars to the heavens.

Fig. 6.4 Writers' images of Jesus and the Spirit

- Christian believers have no doubt that they can and do know God and many read the Scriptures frequently to grow closer to God.

- They attend worship with fellow believers to grow closer to God and many would describe themselves as walking with God or holding God in their hearts or feeling at complete peace and unity with God.

PROGRESS CHECK

1. What is the cosmological argument for the existence of God?
2. What is the point made concerning Paley's watch?
3. What is the numinous?
4. What is a conversion experience?
5. How is God revealed in Christianity?
6. Give two other ways in which God is revealed to Christians.
7. How do Christians reconcile the God of love with the existence of suffering?

1. That God is the first uncaused cause where all that is began. 2. That there must be an intelligent creator God because the universe is clearly designed. 3. An experience of the sacred or the holy. 4. An experience which changes someone's life. 5. In Christianity God is revealed in the person of Jesus. 6. In Christian action and in scripture. 7. By recognising that humans cannot know the fullness of God and must trust in his love and goodness despite suffering.

6.2 Religion and science

 LEARNING SUMMARY

After studying this section you should know and understand:

- *basic views of Christianity towards the origins of the universe*
- *Darwin's theory of evolution*
- *treatment of animals*
- *stewardship*

The origins of the universe

AQA A
OCR B

The big bang theory

In 1948, the Russian-American physicist George Gamow proposed that the universe was created in a gigantic explosion and that the various elements observed today were produced within the first few minutes after the big bang, when the extremely high temperature and density of the universe fused subatomic particles into the chemical elements.

Evolution of the universe

One of the unresolved problems in the expanding universe model is whether the universe is open (that is, whether it will expand forever) or closed (the universe will contract again).

Darwinian theory of evolution

- Charles Darwin explained evolutionary processes in his famous book, *On the Origin of Species by Means of Natural Selection* (1859).
- He noted the differences between offspring and their parents and thought these differences were inherited.
- Animal breeders could change the characteristics of domestic animals by selecting for breeding the most desirable qualities – speed in racehorses, milk production in cows, trail scenting in dogs.
- Darwin assumed that some of a species were better adapted to survive than others, and he called these the fittest, meaning the most suited. When environmental conditions change, populations require new properties to maintain their fitness; the best suited can adapt or change to survive.
- Darwin's theories about the ability to inherit the traits that ensure survival have been seen to have much truth by the 21st century technology that is identifying the human genetic code (DNA).

Make sure you follow the news to find out about the most up-to-date discoveries in human genes.

Humans and animals

- Christians believe that human beings are different from animals but interpretations vary across the Churches and between individuals.

> The Christian tradition asserts that animals have been created by God and that they have an intrinsic value for that reason. Nevertheless, the value of animals has always been seen as secondary to that of human beings made in God's image and placed in a central position in creation. Human beings have both an affinity with and an obligation to animals. (Church of England Board of Social Responsibility)

- The Roman Catholic Church does not teach that animals have human rights.

- The Christian vision is that animals and people exist together in a harmonious world where neither is exploited. (Isaiah 11:6–8).

- In the New Testament, Matthew states that God's covenant is with every living creature and even a sparrow does not die unnoticed. (Matt. 10:29–31)

- Human beings are created in the image of God and animals are not.

KEY POINT — The key Christian idea relating to the treatment of animals is that of stewardship. Mankind is instructed in Genesis to care for God's creation and given stewardship of it.

- The Christian Churches recognise that animal experiments that aim to improve the treatment of human illnesses are acceptable, provided unnecessary suffering is not caused to the animal.

You should be aware that animal rights is one of the most debated issues of current times and look for developing Church teaching about animals.

- Christians are obliged to ensure the comfort and dignity of animals, but do not regard them as equal to human beings.

- Most Christians eat animals as meat or fish, although some might be vegetarian or even vegan (eat or use nothing that contains animal products). Vegetarianism can have a religious foundation but many non-Christians are also vegetarians because of their concern for animals.

PROGRESS CHECK

1. What is the big bang theory?
2. What is Darwin's theory of evolution?
3. According to Christianity, how should animals be treated?
4. Why might a Christian be vegetarian?
5. What is stewardship of animals?

1. The theory that the universe began with an explosion of gases. 2. That human beings have evolved from other species through the survival of the fittest (the most well-adapted to survive). 3. With dignity. 4. Out of respect for God's creation and the view that it is possible to survive without eating meat. 5. Caring for animals as directed by God in the creation story.

6.3 Good and evil

After studying this section you should know and understand:
● **Christian teaching on God and Satan**
● **the Fall**

God and Satan

AQA A
OCR B

- God represents everything that human beings see as good, so He is described in terms of purity, truth, light.

- Satan is the devil, he is the antithesis (opposite) of God and is described in terms of everything that is seen as evil, darkness, deceit, impurity.

- God, the good, is concerned with love, which is the desire to serve others and not to cause pain or harm.

- Satan, the evil, is concerned with hatred, which is the desire to use others, to cause pain and to hurt deliberately.

Christian view of Satan

- The most usual view of Satan is that it is a personification of evil. Christians concentrate the idea of all that is evil into the person of Satan and can target resistance of evil through denying Satan and all his 'works and empty promises' (promises made at baptism).

- It is difficult to imagine Satan as a being, just as it is difficult to imagine God as a being.

- God is personified as a loving Father who watches over his children and all his qualities are shown in the person of Jesus.

- Satan has been represented as a serpent in the story of Adam and Eve. He is drawn as a devil with a tail, carrying a fork and generally red in colour. He is also represented as a goat. All these images are used to convey an idea of the 'evil one'.

- Christians are in no doubt that evil exists and should be resisted. **Christianity is founded on the idea that good (God) has overcome evil for all time through the death and resurrection of Jesus who died to redeem the sin of all humanity.**

The Fall

AQA A
OCR B

- Evil is first noted in the story of Creation in Genesis 2.

- God created Adam and Eve and gave them a perfect garden with only one restriction, not to touch the forbidden fruit.

- Eve was tempted by Satan to offer Adam the fruit of the tree and she and Adam became aware of their nakedness.

- God punished them for their disobedience by throwing them out of the Garden of Eden and condemning them to labour all their lives: Adam to labour on the land and Eve in childbirth.

- Christianity teaches that all humans since that time have been born with **original sin** (the sin of Adam and Eve). All are capable of wrongdoing. (Mary was the only person who conceived without sin, the **Immaculate Conception**.)

- The sin of Adam and Eve and their ejection from Eden is known as **the Fall.**

> **KEY POINT** Humanity was saved from sin (redeemed) by the death and resurrection of Jesus.

Fig. 6.5 A 14th Century depiction of the Crucifixion, painted by Giotto

PROGRESS CHECK

1. How is Satan represented?
2. What is evil?
3. How does God represent good?
4. What is the Fall?
5. What is original sin?
6. How was mankind redeemed?

1. As a serpent, devil or goat. 2. The desire to cause pain, harm or suffering to others. 3. He is described as without any evil, no darkness, only goodness and light. 4. Adam and Eve being expelled from Eden for disobeying God. 5. The sin all humanity bears as a result of the Fall. 6. By the death and resurrection of Jesus.

6.4 Truth and spirituality

LEARNING SUMMARY

After studying this section you should know and understand:

- *that truth is a concept with different interpretations*
- *what constitutes spirituality*

What is truth?

AQA A
OCR B

- People have different understandings of 'truth'.

- Most young children believe that truth is what they think they know is right, e.g. 'I did not hit my friend' could be a truthful statement.

- Most adults know that 'truth' is open to interpretation and one person's truth is another person's untruth. This is especially true with religious claims.

- Some religions claim to be the one true faith or to hold the fullness of truth. This implies that only one religion can really be true and all the others are, therefore, false.

The nature of truth

There are different types of truth.

Scientific truth is based on observing things, such as behaviour and trends in life and science. Scientists construct experiments to test hypotheses (theories) which they devise based on their observations. These theories can be tested and re-tested. Once a hypothesis has been proved by evidence from experiments, a scientist will argue that it is true.

Problem – it is easy to prove a chemical reaction with a scientific test but there are social scientists that experiment with people and these experiments are more difficult to verify. A researcher might ask 100 people if they believe in God and receive these answers:

Yes	35%
No	25%
Not sure	40%

A researcher could ask 100 people, 'Have you ever had an awareness of some sort of transcendent power that some people might call God?' and receive these answers:

Yes	70%
No	15%
Not sure	15%

The scientist might conclude after the last question that it is true that 70 per cent of people believed in God or something that can be described as God. Is this true or is this just one person's version of the truth?

Historical truth is based on evidence from documents and archaeological evidence. Typically, historians believe that a clear picture of historical events can be put together from:

- official documents, such as court records, birth and death certificates and letters

- archaeological evidence

- eyewitness accounts and interviews

- news reports from the time

- accounts of other historians who have studied the evidence

Problem – if two people witness exactly the same event, they will record it differently so even documents and eyewitness accounts can only give one perspective. With historical events, people have their own interpretations, which become their own 'truth'.

Moral truth is derived from ideas of right and wrong and conclusions are reached by abstract reasoning.

Abstract ideas are drawn from concrete or real events. An example would be the view that all people are born with the potential to be evil or to do each other harm. This is an abstract idea that can be concluded by observing human behaviour.

Spiritual truth is a matter for private individual faith. Each religious tradition teaches its own truth based on religious authority, such as the religious leaders or the scriptures.

Within each religious tradition, individual believers interpret the teachings of the authorities and the scriptures. They interpret these things according to their own **conscience.**

> **KEY POINT**
>
> **Conscience is the inner voice that speaks inside each person informing them of right and wrong. It is formed by teaching and by the internal knowledge of God, which is part of each person (according to Christian teaching).**

The spiritual is that part of the human person that searches for a deeper meaning in life. It is the part that engages with **questions of meaning**, which are:

● Where did I come from?

● Where am I going?

● Why am I here?

Acknowledging the spiritual dimension means recognising that there is another dimension to life other than the concrete and tangible (what you can see and touch).

The spiritual dimension is concerned with those thoughts and feelings that fill people with awe and wonder and a sense of mystery. It can be a deep sense of peace when confronted with scenes of great natural beauty or even magnificent human achievements, the triumph of the human spirit.

Understanding spirituality

AQA A
OCR B

People can gain insight into spirituality by:

● exploring creativity in art, music, drama, dance, literature, sport, design or any other area that causes people to draw on their emotions and feelings to achieve beauty and meaning in their work

● taking part in activities that afford opportunities to draw on inner strength or spirituality that help people to know themselves better, to know their strengths and weaknesses – this can assist in developing feelings of self worth and high self-esteem

● becoming more self aware through exploring emotions and spiritual dimensions, which can also promote greater awareness of the feelings and beliefs of others

Candidates might refer to athletes, such as Jonathan Edwards or Kriss Akabusi, who have indicated faith in God and use of talents in His service as inspiration for their achievements.

For Christians and other religious believers, the experience of the spiritual is inextricably linked with the experience of God.

● God is the spiritual dimension for religious believers.

● God is the inspiration within human creativity because He is the creator, therefore all Christians dedicate their creativity to the service of God.

● God is evident in all creation and in all human achievement. In beauty and greatness, Christians encounter God and spirituality.

● Experience of God builds spiritual truth for believers.

Fig. 6.6 Jonathan Edwards triple-jumping

Religious truth

It is true that most children go to school. It is true that most children sit GCSEs at the end of Year 11. It is true that fire is hot.

Some statements seem simple and most people do not disagree with the truth of what all can witness.

Truth in religion is very complex. Each religion has its own scriptures, rituals, ethics, symbols, stories, traditions and dogmas. Each has its own truth.

KEY POINT

Within each religious tradition individual members have their own truth. Religious belief is based on faith. Faith begins where reason stops. Ultimately religious believers believe in something beyond the tangible and material. Christians call this God.

PROGRESS CHECK

1. List four different types of truth.
2. On what is historical truth based?
3. What is abstract reasoning?
4. What is a hypothesis?
5. How do people arrive at their own spiritual truth within religion?
6. What is spirituality?

1. Scientific, historical, spiritual and moral. 2. On documentary and archaeological evidence. 3. Principles deduced from concrete experience and then applied to other arguments. 4. A theory that can be scientifically tested. 5. From religious authority, sacred writings and individual conscience. 6. A dimension to human existence which goes beyond the tangible and material.

Sample GCSE questions

1. **Truth and spirituality**

Read the following statements and then answer the questions below.

Statement A   I'm religious. My holy book and my conscience tell me what's true.

Statement B   The only truth is what science can prove. Belonging to a religion is a waste of time.

Statement C   There's more to life than science can prove. People are more than just machines. I'm not religious but I think we all have a spiritual side.

(a)   Look at Statement A. Give one example of a holy book.   **(1)**

The Bible (The Qur´an, the Tanach)

(b)   Look at Statement A. What is meant by conscience?   **(2)**

An inner voice formed by inherent knowledge of good and evil and developed by moral or religious upbringing. Possibly an internal dialogue with God or a moral awareness of right and wrong.

> *Candidates should learn the definition of conscience from their own religious viewpoint but will be credited for expressing the ideas shown here in their own words.*

(c)   Look at Statement B. How does science prove something is true?   **(4)**

Science sets about to prove something is true by formulating a hypothesis and establishing a test to prove the hypothesis. It has established protocols, such as `fair testing´, `random sampling´ and `representative samples´, to eliminate as much error as possible. The results of the test are then matched to the hypothesis and the conclusion is drawn as to the truth or otherwise of the hypothesis.

> *There is no one answer to this question. You should make sure you read the description of social science experiments as well as the suggested answer, and also apply knowledge from your own study of science.*

(d)   Look at Statement B. How would a religious believer argue against the idea that belonging to a religion is a waste of time?   **(4)**

Religious believers gain a great deal from belonging to religious communities. The first benefit for them is the individual relationship with God, and the faith and hope that guide and direct every part of their lives. This faith is strengthened by being part of a praying community in private, group and corporate worship. The spiritual bonds of believers are cemented by practical benefits for communities. They meet together sharing the same ideals and values. They give each other practical and emotional support in times of crisis. They work together to fulfil their charitable obligations to the needy as their witness to faith in the world.

> *This is an AO2 question so you need to describe, analyse and explain the relevance of religion.*

Sample GCSE questions

(e) Look at a Statement C. Explain why it might be said that all people have a spiritual side. **(4)**

> *Every person is capable of appreciating greatness, great beauty, great achievement and the sense that comes from seeing the extraordinary. On witnessing extraordinary things, people are filled with a sense of awe and wonder and it is this sense that causes humans to ask ultimate questions about the meaning of life. Achieving greatness and feeling inspired helps to develop self-esteem and self-worth.*

This question is about understanding spirituality and not necessarily about having any sort of belief in a deity.

(f) 'The only truth is what science can prove.'
Do you agree? Give reasons for your answer, showing that you have thought about more than one point of view. **(5)**

> *A scientist might say that all truth has to be scientifically proven by providing evidence of a hypothesis that has been properly tested under strict conditions. However, there are some things that can never be scientifically proven, such as the existence of God, but does that mean that God is not true or belief in God is not real?*
>
> *Religious believers base their belief in God on many types of evidence: on historical evidence, moral and ethical argument and especially on personal experience of God. For people who experience God in a profound way in worship or in some other kind of spiritual fulfilment, God is true.*
>
> *Even some scientists recognise that scientific truth is only valid temporarily as knowledge grows. Once it was believed that the world was flat but this was later proved to be untrue.*

This is an AO3 question, which means you have to evaluate different responses to religious and moral issues. You have to use the information that is given in this chapter.

AQA Syllabus B Specimen Paper

Exam practice answers

Chapter 1 Christianity

1. Beliefs and values

(a) Son of God/Saviour of Mankind/Redeemer

(b) Maker of Heaven and Earth, Father Almighty

(c) Repentance is essential for forgiveness of sins; repentance implies willingness to reform; repentance means sorrow for the harm which has been caused. Faith means complete trust and safe understanding of God's willingness to forgive and to look after a Christian at all times and to love unconditionally even when he is rejected by the faithful.

(d) Non Christians can:
- help others
- give to charity
- work for the needy
- preserve the environment
- live a good life causing nobody any hurt or pain

Christians can:
- fail constantly to live the life
- be selfish
- hurt others
- fail to be charitable
- go to church and still cause others pain

2. Organisation

(a) The laity are ordinary non-ordained members of a Christian community.

(b) Bible is read aloud in church by laity and ministers, reflected on, prayed with, interpreted in sermons.

(c) Church means the people of God, not just the building and hierarchy. The lives of good men and women who have been witness to Christianity through selfless actions and acts of sacrifice help the faithful. Constant prayer and practice build faith.

(d) A Christian is a follower of Jesus and Jesus is clear that Christianity involves service to others in some way. Even contemplative religious people serve each other in some way. A life of total isolation is not possible. A young Christian amongst many non-Christians might feel alone but Christians are never alone, they are always with others and with God.

Chapter 2 The Gospels

1. Short answer questions

(a) Good News

(b) Matthew and Luke

(c) He was tempted by the devil.

(d) Moses and Elijah

(e) He was a Samaritan.

(f) The Last Supper

(g) Jesus' ascent into heaven

(h) Because he did it on the Sabbath.

(i) By devoting their lives to serving God and not to amassing wealth.

(j) That God is always ready to welcome people back when they turn to him.

(k) Christians have undertaken missionary work in many countries of the world, preaching the Word of God and baptising people.

(l) That Jesus founded his Church on a solid foundation and that the Petrine line is the continuum of the Church.

(m) Jesus knew he would be betrayed; someone had to do this. Peter denied Jesus but went on to serve him and be a martyr in his name, so Jesus was not a bad judge of character.

Exam practice answers

Chapter 4 Social issues

1. Prejudice and discrimination

(a) All mankind are created equal by God. There is no Jew or Gentile, no slave or free, no man or woman according to St Paul. In Leviticus Christians are taught when there is a stranger in your land, treat him as one of your own. Christianity teaches that this is wrong to treat a person differently because of their race. In St Paul's letter to Philemon, he begs him to treat the one-time slave Onesimus justly and fairly.

These teachings are important for Catholics today because they remind them to welcome strangers especially with the degree of migration that there is between countries. In the UK there are asylum seekers and refugees who need to be welcomed and this is difficult in the face of criticism about financial burden and taxation. Catholics should be at the forefront of condemning acts of genocide such as those in Kosovo and Rwanda and East Timor. The biblical teachings remind Catholics of the obligation to welcome all races as Christ in their midst.

(b) By taking a person of another race under his roof; by having a personal relationship with someone of another race; by making friends with people of other races; by endorsing and enforcing equal opportunities policies at school, in the workplace and in society. As employers by positively discriminating on behalf of those who might be victims of prejudice, such as women, the disabled, the unemployed, homosexuals, the mentally handicapped and people of ethnic minorities.

This would be based on following the Christian teaching which instructs Christians to feed the hungry, clothe the naked, visit the imprisoned, comfort the lonely, and on the teaching of St Paul and in Leviticus. It is also based on the teaching of the World Council of Churches which says everyone is created in the image of Christ and racism is an assault on Christ's values and his sacrifice for the human race.

(c) Christianity is quite clear that women and men are equal. All people are created unique by God, in his image. He created man and woman to complement each other. St Paul teaches that men and women are equal. This does not mean they are the same. Women bear children and feed them. Men are biologically different. Generally men are potentially stronger than women: they can run faster, lift heavier weights and develop greater strength on average than women. Men and women are individuals with individual skills and talents, all of which are needed in a diverse and creative world. They are equal but not the same.

2. Life and death

(a) Catholicism teaches that when a person dies they might have to undergo a period of purification known as purgatory before they attain the beatific vision of God. People that reject God by hate, cruelty and sin eternally separate themselves from Him in Hell. All will be judged according to the way they have lived their lives and are obliged to follow the teachings that Jesus gave them to care for the poor. On the day of judgement all deeds will be revealed and those who have denied God and rejected him will be sent away. At the end of time the Kingdom of God will come in its fullness and the righteous will reign with Christ, glorified in body and soul (Catechism of the Catholic Church).

(b) The Roman Catholic Church teaches quite clearly that euthanasia is unlawful killing and goes against the Christian life. All life is sacred, created by God in his image and each person has a dignity, which should be inviolable. Euthanasia can offend against human dignity. Roman Catholicism also teaches that it is wrong to take extraordinary measures to preserve life. A Christian spouse would endeavour to preserve life and preserve dignity by ensuring the spouse had the best possible medical care to control pain and ensure a good quality of life to the end. A Christian spouse would try to ensure palliative care of the best quality.

(c) A funeral for a Catholic family is a religious rite that marks the end of the earthly journey. It affords the opportunity for the family and the community to pray for the soul of the dear departed and publicly affirm their faith in eternal life. The family is brought together with the community of which it is part; they are all reminded of their own mortality and the fragility of material things, the need to pay attention to the commandments. It also reminds the whole family of their part in the unfolding Christian story of the community of saints and all holy men and women who have gone before marked with the sign of faith. So, it is one of the most important occasions for a Catholic family.

Index

Index